The Archer Method of Winning at 21

JOHN ARCHER

1977 EDITION

Published by
Melvin Powers
WILSHIRE BOOK COMPANY
12015 Sherman Road
No. Hollywood, California 91605
Telephone: (213) 875-1711

Library of Congress Cataloging in Publication Data
Archer, John, 1923-
The Archer method of winning at twenty-one.

Includes bibliographical references.
1. Twenty-One (Game) I. Title.
GV1295.B55A7   795.4'2   73-6449

Printed by

HAL LEIGHTON PRINTING CO.
P.O. Box 1231
Beverly Hills, California 90213
Telephone: (213) 983-1105

Published by Henry Regnery Company
114 West Illinois Street, Chicago, Illinois 60610
Manufactured in the United States of America
Library of Congress Catalog Card Number: 73-6449

ISBN 0-87980-328-2

To Dora, Linda, and Diana —
with affection and appreciation for
much help and patience, including the dealing
of several hundred thousand
practice hands.

Contents

Introduction
An Odd Thing Happened
to the Game of Blackjack

LATE one night in Reno, I walked through the small casino in my hotel, went to the desk in the lobby, and asked for my deposit box. The young clerk took the key and started toward the depository, but then he hesitated. "Do you want to take it all out or just part of it?"

The "it," namely the money in the box, was exclusively my property, so I asked, "What difference does that make?"

He was polite. "The weekend's coming up, and we'll be busy. If you're taking it all out, we can give the box to someone else."

I was slightly annoyed. "I'll still need the box. Just let me have the thing." I realized from the young man's countenance that I had sounded rude. As a kind of apology, I went on to acknowledge something that was none of his proper concern: "Actually, I want to put some in."

The boy showed delighted astonishment. "Oh. Certainly. That doesn't happen here very often."

ix

Obviously it had not happened to this young man before. The casinos in Nevada—and everywhere else—are operated to take a visitor's money like boll weevils take cotton.

But *I* win. I gamble in casinos and win consistently—not at every session but consistently overall. And I have taught a few other people to do the same thing. This book can teach any normally intelligent reader how to walk into a prestigious gambling casino and beat the professionals at their own game.

I refer to the game of Blackjack, or Twenty-One. Among the games played in modern casinos, this one is unique by offering a skilled player the opportunity to compete against the house and have a statistical probability of winning. The design of all other games gives the casino a mathematical advantage by providing payoffs of players' winning bets in amounts slightly or greatly less than the true odds would require.

As a single example, a winning bet on one number at roulette pays 35 to 1 (or 36 *for* 1). Since 38 numbers are present on the American wheel, a payoff at true odds would require 37 to 1. Thus, on a single turn of the wheel, if the players should bet an equal unit amount on every number, the casino would return 36 units for the number that won and retain 2 units for itself as profit.

While the house percentage varies from game to game, and usually between the bets that are possible on the same game, all bets on the layouts for roulette, craps, baccarat, chuck-a-luck, the money wheel, and the big six involve such a percentage. The slot machines and keno, in the long run, return a smaller amount to the players than is deposited in the slots or at the keno counter. While in theory a studious player might detect some mechanical bias or defect that would allow him to overcome his mathematical disadvantage at some of these games, the casinos are diligent in their efforts to prevent any imperfections in their equipment.

Games such as poker and pan might appear to be exceptions to the concept that Blackjack is unique; a skillful player of these games might reasonably expect to beat his opponents. But poker and pan are played against other players, not against the casino; the casino's profit comes from a fee the dealer cuts from the pots. Bingo is analogous. On rare but conceivable occasions the number of players might be so small that a game providing a fixed payoff could return a larger sum to the winner than the casino collected on that particular game. But here, too, the players are really competing against each other, not against the house.

Since a casino is in business to make money, the reader might ask why it would provide a game that can be beaten. The answer is twofold. For one thing, the overwhelming majority of players does not have the knowledge and skill to beat the game or even to come close. Thus, Blackjack is still profitable, overall, to the house. Also, it is probable that when the game was installed, the casino managers did not realize that the game would leave them vulnerable to defeat.

The history of the game is obscure. It seems to have evolved from one or a variety of similar games long played in Europe. It was known in this country during the last century and became popular during the early twentieth century. Variations have been played extensively in the armed forces for years, and Blackjack has enjoyed considerable popularity in clubs and homes and at private parties. Over the years the game has developed into one of the most popular of all casino games.

The precise rules of the casino version of Blackjack must have been developed empirically as the proprietors sought to provide themselves an advantage yet to offer the player an interesting game that seemed to give the player some prospect of winning. A game that took a player's money too fast or that failed to provide him with occasional short winning streaks would soon drive him to another diversion. But unlike dice games, wheel games, lotteries, and some card games, Blackjack did not lend itself to calculation· of a precise overall house percentage; among other difficulties, this could be calculated only if all players acted consistently, which they did not. Thus, the casinos settled for an estimated advantage, based upon their average income from an approximate amount of money wagered, or "action." As profits were good and the tables remained crowded, with almost no players seeming to win consistently, the casinos were pleased. Within all this lay the germ of a remarkable episode in casino history that was to develop in recent years: the emergence of a small class of players who could come into the casinos and put the *house* at a disadvantage.

I should mention now that the term *blackjack* is somewhat of a misnomer. The jack of spades and jack of clubs no longer are treated as different from other face cards and 10s. Historically and logically, the alternate designation of *Twenty-One* is preferable, and I will use it from this point on in the book. The term *blackjack* will be reserved for a specific combination of cards (and even for this, the term *natural* is a more proper designation than *blackjack*).

The Unique Game

One facet of the uniqueness of Twenty-One is that a player can make decisions in the manner of play that influence the outcome of the game. This feature is absent from all other games in which the player contests the house. Other games do offer options, and thus decisions, in the types of *bets* the player may make. But once a bet is placed, a player has no discretionary control over whether he wins or loses. A craps player may roll the dice and thus, in a sense, determine the outcome, but he has no conscious influence over what total the dice will show. The entire matter rests on chance. (Admittedly, a player might develop a technique of manipulating the roll of the dice, but casino personnel are constantly on the lookout for any such illegal maneuvers.)

Further, Twenty-One is the only casino game in which the outcome of one betting transaction depends in any predictable way upon what has transpired during previous transactions. By contrast, the number that appears with a roll of dice or spin of a wheel is uninfluenced by the previous play—or the previous thousand plays. Much money has been lost through a superstitious belief that some number, or perhaps some combination on a slot machine, was "due to hit" simply because it had not recently appeared. A similar fallacy is the notion that some number is "lucky" because it has appeared a few times with uncommon frequency. Except in the event of some unusual mechanical bias, any one number on a roulette wheel, for example, has precisely one chance in 38 of appearing on the next spin, whether it has appeared half a dozen times or not at all on the preceding 100; a craps player has exactly one chance in six of making a 7 on his next roll, and one in 36 of making, say, a 12, regardless of how long ago or how recently he has made either. The dice, the roulette wheel, and the slot machine have no memory. The odds are self-restoring.

But at Twenty-One, after any number of cards have been dealt, the composition of the remaining, undealt portion of the deck virtually always has an abnormal composition in comparison with that of a full deck in terms of the ratio of cards of varying rank to one another. Since more than one round of hands is usually dealt before the cards are shuffled together again, the cards appearing on one round will give an indication of those that are more likely to appear on the next. Expert players can use the information obtained by observing the cards played to increase their chances of winning. The purpose of this book is to make you such an expert.

If you fear from what you have just read that I am going to ask you to remember every card you see played, do not despair. *I* certainly could never accomplish such a feat, and few people can. In fact, you can play successfully without remembering *any* specific cards. Insofar as the count of the cards is concerned, you will need to remember only *one* number, easily derived, at any given time.* Once I have taught you (in Chapter 3) to derive that number, I will present a series of logical ways to use it in playing the hands you may be dealt.

Development of the Scientific Game

Well before the elaborate mathematical data were perfected to provide fully scientific Twenty-One strategies, some players developed methods of their own for winning play based upon a memory of cards. The exploits of a few such players are recounted in legend, and others have probably been forgotten. Surely, some of these early experts used a combination of statistics and logical thinking to develop their techniques. Just how close they came to ideal play, as later derived with the aid of electronic computers, is uncertain. But conditions in the casinos before computer technology invaded the game would not have required play nearly as sophisticated as is necessary now. Almost

---

*One lone exception, an advanced refinement, will be discussed in Chapter 9. There you will learn to improve your efficiency by remembering a second number.

certainly, much of the success of the pioneer winners involved the use of *end play:* when only a few cards remained to be dealt at the end of a deck, a memory of the previous cards would sometimes reveal a composition highly favorable to the player; in this circumstance a very large bet would be made. (For reasons to be discussed in later chapters, opportunities for highly aggressive end play are less common today. But there are other ways to win.)

These early virtuosos were probably little more than a mild annoyance to the casinos. The beginning of the real onslaught of players against the casinos was essentially unheralded when, in 1956, four mathematicians published in the scientific literature a revolutionary strategy for Twenty-One, which would give any player an approximately even chance at the game.[1] These were Roger Baldwin, Wilbert Cantey, Herbert Maisel, and James McDermott. Their product was the result of long and diligent research, using manually operated calculators. A year later, in a book now out of print, they published their findings for the general public.[2]

The initial strategy of the Baldwin group did not involve card counting but assumed that all hands were dealt from a full (52-card) deck. The authors did not claim that theirs was a winning strategy, but they said that it would provide the player with the best possible *chance* to win, taking no account of any abnormal compositions of the deck. Despite the limitations of this system, its publication represented a landmark event in the history of casino gambling. For one thing, it inspired further study. For another, it provided the first scientifically derived, verifiable technique for the ordinary player to confront a casino on essentially *even* terms.

Instead of claiming that their strategy gave the player an even game, the Baldwin group calculated that the house would still have a fraction of a percent advantage. However, later examination detected an error in this calculation and demonstrated that a player using the Baldwin strategy would have approximately an even bet. In fact, with the moderately more liberal rules then in effect, he might have had a slight statistical advantage!

The Baldwin strategy has been repeatedly confirmed by other authors and mathematicians, who have made only minor corrections and added slight refinements.[3-12] With moderate changes, the Baldwin method still represents the *basic* strategy for expert, card-counting players who vary their method of play according to the composition of a partially depleted deck.

The Baldwin group recognized the potential value of taking into account the cards dealt to previous hands, but they did not develop a refined technique of doing so.[7] In their original paper, they seemed to regard use of such information as too difficult for practical application. Other mathematicians thought differently. One such scientist has had an impact on the game equivalent to that of Goren on bridge and the forward pass on football. In 1961 Dr. Edward O. Thorp[3,4] published in the scientific literature a winning strategy for Twenty-One, which he derived with the aid of an IBM computer. His method was based on a confirmation (with minor corrections) of the Baldwin strategy and on a variation of this strategy, according to formula, as indicated by the composition of cards remaining in the partially depleted deck. At the same time the player would vary the size of bets, making them large when prospects were favorable and small when they were not.

Soon afterward a series of books appeared that presented a wide variety of mathematically sound techniques that, if employed properly, would provide a statistical advantage to the Twenty-One player against the dealer. The most important of these were *Beat the Dealer* by Thorp,[5,6] *The Casino Gambler's Guide* by Dr. Allan Wilson,[7] *The Theory of Gambling and Statistical Logic* by Richard Epstein,[8] and, more recently, *Playing Blackjack as a Business* by Lawrence Revere.[9] Among these, Epstein's book is technically the most thorough in describing and analyzing numerous winning systems; the presentation, however, is highly intricate and difficult to follow. Wilson's book is very readable and perhaps contains more general and practical advice than the others. Revere's book is more compact but contains some gems of advice that are more contemporary. Thorp's books, particularly if considered together, describe more systems than do Wilson and Revere (but fewer than Epstein).

Thorp was first to publish and has received by far the most public attention. In fact, when his *Beat the Dealer* achieved its greatest notice, in 1964, the casinos on the Las Vegas Strip went so far as to change the rules of the game in an effort to counteract the effect of the new strategy. Fortunately, the changes were only temporary. A sudden lack of business forced the casinos to restore the previous rules. The casinos overreacted to the threat anyway; the really powerful strategies in the book were far too difficult for any but a handful of players to master.

I also know of a few individuals who have privately developed sound systems, either by making independent computer analyses or by adapting available published data to applications they find most convenient. Despite the undetermined number of such systems, they all can be reduced to three basic types: rank-count systems, point-count systems, and the 10-count system.

A rank-count system was first presented in the scientific literature by Thorp. The technique merely involves counting the cards of a single rank and making appropriate adjustments in play if that rank becomes depleted, taking into account the composition of the player's hand and what is known about the dealer's hand.*

Such a system is fairly easy, but unfortunately the profits gained by this system are almost negligible. The impact of Thorp's invention was not as much from the effectiveness of the system as from the fact that it was the first to promise *some* statistical advantage, however slight, to the player. Thorp's rank count involved 5s: it may surprise many people familiar with Twenty-One that the seemingly nondescript 5, in its own way, is more important than any other single card. Revere also describes the 5-count system. With characteristic thoroughness, Epstein presents a rank-count strategy for every card in the deck; as they now stand, however, these data appear to be more of academic interest than of practical use.

Most systems involve some type of point count. As cards are dealt, the player mentally assigns positive numerical values to cards of certain ranks and negative values to others; thus he arrives at an algebraic sum, which continues to fluctuate as the game proceeds. Depending upon this sum (point count) at any moment of decision, he varies the size of bets, the strategy for playing hands, or both, according to the formula for the particular system in use. The effectiveness of these systems thus far presented varies roughly according to the difficulty of mastering them. Those theoretically promising a really high yield of profit require a mental agility far greater than the simplistic description I have just given would suggest. They require simultaneous counts of more than one type and rapid mental calculations to

---

*To readers who have never played Twenty-One, these details may seem obscure at the moment, but an explanation of the game is given in Chapter 1.

integrate these and convert them to a meaningful result. Only the rarest individual has the computer-like brain to make such counts and calculations in the midst of a casino's fast play. Ordinary mortals can, with practice, play some of the less demanding point-count methods described in the books I have mentioned, but these provide only modest profits.*

From its name, the 10-count system might appear to be another rank-count system. However, the designation *10 count* is slightly misleading. The system, first described to the public by Thorp, involves counting cards to derive the arithmetic ratio of non-10 pip cards to the combined 10s and face cards that remain in the undealt deck.

The 10-count system is a powerful weapon against the casinos for the individual who can master it, but such mental acrobats must be exceedingly rare. Simultaneous and rapid counts of the number of cards played and the number of certain ranks among these, together with repeated recalculations of the arithmetic ratio of one count to another, constitute a formidable task alone. But the system also involves applying this ratio appropriately to any of hundreds of different card combinations. Thus, it is easy to understand why, despite the ready availability to the public of this system, the profits of the casinos have remained secure.

The intent of this discussion is not to review the literature on Twenty-One but to summarize briefly the advent of scientifically derived strategies that provide a statistical advantage to the player sufficiently adept to use them. I should mention, however, that an array of potboilers has

---

*The preceding generalization may do a slight injustice to Lawrence Revere, and I want to avoid that. Revere presents one obviously powerful point-count system that an intelligent person should be able to master if he works hard enough; but the system is by no means easy.

continued to appear, purporting to give advice on Twenty-One, that can only insure a continued flow of money into the casinos' counting rooms. Such offerings contain unsound strategies, superstitions, contradictions, and farragoes of nonsense. A few entrepreneurs have advertised Twenty-One systems for sale by mail order. Revere's book delivers a scathing indictment of these products. Certain inferior but popular books admittedly may present strategies that are superior to what an untutored player might develop empirically. But they can only lead him to lose more slowly than otherwise, not to win.

A few exceptions to those presentations should be noted in addition to the books previously named. A little book by Charles Einstein[10] gives a counting system of intermediate difficulty that involves bet variation and a moderate amount of strategy variation. I believe the author probably overestimated the player's advantage with the system. Employed correctly, however, it will win, and the author wrote with a keen insight into the game. Somewhat unbecoming, however, is Einstein's subtle disparagement of Dr. Edward Thorp, who pioneered winning Twenty-One systems.

Considered in tandem, two books by Donald Collver[13] and Robert Scharff[11] are interesting and could be valuable to a student of Twenty-One. Collver is an engineer and former dealer of the game who developed a system that dictates an elaborate strategy variation as the count changes. His basic strategy is slightly eccentric, but only in minor ways. Most surprising, he paid only superficial attention to the important matter of sound bet variation. Scharff described a similar counting technique, the more conventional basic strategy (except for one lapse when he contradicted himself), and a good system of bet variation. However, he gave only a bit of general advice on varying the play of the hands as the count changes. If the best features of each of these two books are extracted and combined, a fairly difficult but reasonably effective system emerges.

Finally, *Oswald Jacoby on Gambling*,[12] published in 1963, must be mentioned. The author, a veteran gambler, mathematician, and writer on card games, calculated the basic strategy with only minor variations from that of the Baldwin group. He added a valid but cursory presentation of a 10-count strategy almost devoid of details yet still containing enough to provide an advantage to the player over the casino. Then, irony arose: a few pages later the author firmly proclaimed that no amount of skill could give the player an expectation of winning at a casino game; apparently he had described a winning system without knowing he had done so.

By the time Jacoby's pronouncement appeared in print, it was, of course, anachronistic. Thorp had already proved publicly that winning systems were possible. And almost simultaneously, Harvey Dubner* was describing to a scientific meeting still another one.

Another Winning Method Evolves

I have long been a student of games, and years ago I became fascinated by casino gambling. At the time I would play a bit, but never heavily; I understood the percentages involved and realized that any real hope of eventually winning was futile—at least then. Nevertheless, I enjoyed the excitement of the games, the slight prospect at least of a temporary run of luck, and the peripheral, inexpensive luxuries to be found—either at such great resorts as Las Vegas, or in a fabulous club like the old Balinese Room

---

*Dubner did not publish, but his point-count system is described by others.[6,8] In similar vein, Julian Braun's basic mathematical data have contributed enormously to scientific Twnety-One.[6-9]

in Galveston. I preferred craps, confining myself to the line bets and the "come" or "don't come," which I knew to be the best bets in the casinos (and they still are unless a player is an expert at Twenty-One).

At that time, I played Twenty-One only enough to be convinced that it was an unattractive game, although it did occur to me that a player who could remember cards would be able to improve his decisions on whether to stand, draw, double down, or split certain pairs. At a very early period, I even devoted some time to calculating a basic strategy.

However, I did not pursue the matter at the time; craps was my game. This occasional pastime was only moderately expensive and well worth that for the entertainment. But anyone who gambles wants to win. And in view of that desire, the revelations of the mathematicians that Twenty-One could be beaten was a prodigy. The perfected basic strategy alone was enough to give the player essentially an equal chance, and systems began to appear that actually gave the player an advantage. Until then I had thought that anyone who seriously imagined such a thing about casino gambling must have been a fool or a larcenist. But a respect for science and mathematics and a study of the systems soon overcame my prejudice. I first set out to learn Thorp's method. I can say honestly that I had no plans to make any real profit at the enterprise. For one thing, I no longer lived near a casino at that time. I simply wanted to be able, when I did have the opportunity, to engage in my occasional hobby and to leave the tables a few dollars ahead more often than losing. I often had gambled in casinos for amusement with the recognition that I would probably lose, and if necessary, I had every intention of continuing to do it again now and then. But why not do the same thing with the probability of winning? It would certainly be more fun.

I learned the 5-count strategy fairly well and used it a bit. But this system provides only a trivial yield. Inevitably, I should want to play the much more powerful 10-count strategy. After some preliminary effort, however, a disagreeable realization unfolded: I simply was not able to master it. I could understand the principles, and I thought that eventually I would be able to memorize the various strategy decisions that must be made for the hundreds of types of possible card combinations. But there remained the necessity of mentally calculating and recalculating the ratio of non-10s to 10s in the remaining deck, under the conditions of the fast casino game, and applying the data simultaneously to any of these many combinations. That task seemed overwhelming.*

Since I could not master this strategy, I began some innovating of my own. I began to seek a shortcut, a key, some reliable index for deriving a useful approximation of the ratio of non-10s to 10s without the necessity of constantly keeping mental account of the exact number of each of the two ranks remaining in the deck and mentally dividing one total into the other. A simple point-count *index* to the ratio was the result. My invention is the only really easy method I have seen described to derive the exact or closely approximate 10 count. It does not involve dealing with ratios per se but only with a point-count figure. Not only does it *greatly* simplify the 10 count, but it also is inherently easier to keep than *any* point count I have seen. If you learn it, you will win.

While my point-count method represented a prodigious

---

* I find some consolation in Allan Wilson's discussion of the 10-count strategy. Even though he presented it in his excellent book, he wrote candidly about the formidable difficulty of applying the method in actual play. Since this pioneer expert also found the 10 count extraordinarily trying, I no longer felt so bad.

breakthrough in simplifying the 10 count, its discovery was only the beginning of my work. Use of the count to full advantage often requires that the cards be played in one manner with one count and in another manner with a different count. Thus, there remained the need not only to reduce playing strategies appropriate for specific ratios to corresponding point counts, but also to devise a format that would be practical to learn and use.

I spent my spare time for more than two years in studying, making calculations, experimenting, verifying details, and organizing material to produce a system that sacrificed only little in accuracy while lending itself to practical application. Four additional years have gone into revising, refining, further simplifying, and writing about the system. With little loss of precision, I have succeeded in reducing the major points of decision for strategy changes from 45 to only 8. I also have devised strategies and techniques never presented in any other book that I have seen. During this period I have played Twenty-One often and in many casinos to test the system, to add practical application to theory, and to gather material for this book. After the system was sufficiently developed and I had gained some experience, I compiled an impressive winning record at the tables. Thus, what began as a diversion came to involve a substantial amount of work but also to provide something more tangible than recreation. I have taught the system to any of my friends who were sufficiently interested to learn, and they too have gone on to win.

Study the Method and Play to Win

While the obvious intent of any serious student and player of Twenty-One is to win, his more basic motives are, in my opinion, personal. Although I began to play and develop my system as a hobby, I learned that I could play for fairly high stakes and win, which made the pastime even more worthwhile. Yet I still would not play unless I enjoyed doing so. The one way I can unequivocally recommend the game to you is that you play for enjoyment. If you are excited by the prospect of being an expert, of making continuous, rapid, devastatingly accurate decisions at a fascinating game, Blackjack is for you.

Of course, it *is* possible to make money at playing Twenty-One. Particularly if you live near the casinos, and thus have no problem of major overhead expense, your gambling capital can be almost your total investment, and winnings will be nearly all profit. But even in this circumstance, I think you should find the game entertaining; otherwise, the time involved might better be spent at a less risky enterprise. Regardless of your statistical advantage, the game is still a gamble, and there is no guarantee of winning. If playing involves a high overhead for transportation and dislocated living, prospects of a true profit will require playing for rather high stakes and the risk of a large gambling capital.

To summarize, mine is a winning method, and it can be mastered by the studious, intelligent reader. I present a system that will give you a mathematical probability of winning *something* when you play. Whether you strive to win a large sum or just a bit is your personal decision. I have only three fundamental recommendations: master the method described in the remainder of this book; enjoy the game; and never gamble with money you cannot afford to lose.

To Learn the Method

The format of this book is didactic. While playing Twenty-One is easy in a fashion, there is absolutely no easy way to learn to play it *well*. I have designed the presentation of my method to make it as easy to learn as I could, but you will still have to study to master it.

With the habits of a teacher, I have organized the chapters much like a series of lessons. The content of each largely assumes a knowledge of the preceding. I follow the teacher's instinct of believing that discourse must not only give essential facts but explanations to lead the student to understand the facts. Occasionally, for logical sequence, I present relatively unimportant details in conjunction with what is vital; but when I do, I usually designate what can be deferred for later review.

I suggest frequent practice sessions during the first and subsequent excursions through the book. I say *subsequent* because I know that a real mastery of the method will require rereading and restudy. The summaries in certain chapters will make review easier. If possible, have a friend deal to you when you practice. The more nearly you can simulate the conditions of casino play, the better. But if necessary, deal hands to yourself and the nonexistent dealer.

If you have played a bit of Twenty-One but never before have studied the game seriously, you may be surprised by some of the recommended tactics. We now know to do things that once would have been considered gross folly. Accordingly, I suggest that you read carefully the reasons that accompany many of the recommendations. These will give you confidence in following certain tactics that seem to run counter to initial instincts. One of the fascinations of the game is that expert play requires techniques that sometimes astonish the uninitiated.

A Word of Caution—A Word of Reassurance

One unfortunate facet of Twenty-One must be recognized: the game is particularly amenable to cheating by the dealer.

This sordid subject will be discussed in some detail in Chapter 10. At the moment, it is sufficient to note that in a legally sanctioned casino subject to government surveillance and regulation as in Nevada, the danger of cheating in any given game is small. A casino has both a license and a reputation to protect. Nevertheless, the danger of occasionally being cheated does exist. If you follow the advice I will offer in Chapter 10, you can protect yourself reasonably well.

1

How the Game is Played

ALTHOUGH all games of Twenty-One are fundamentally similar, the one played in the casinos varies in important ways from that frequently played in amateur sessions. Thus, the reader who is not intimately familiar with casino play should read this chapter carefully before making an effort to master the other parts of the book. I suggest that even those who have played a bit in casinos but not extensively or in a variety of places also read the chapter for a review and perhaps a few details that they may have missed previously.

A friend who read an early draft of this book criticized what he regarded as a provincial preoccupation with Nevada in general and Las Vegas in particular. After all, casino Twenty-One is played in many other parts of the world.

Nevertheless, I have good reason for concentrating on the Las Vegas game in this presentation. First, a fairly consistent set of rules prevails there, and these rules can be regarded as a good standard against which all other games can be compared. The few variations in rules that do occur in Las Vegas casinos are quite easy to point out. Collectively, the Las Vegas rules embrace most of the important and common players' options in managing hands that may be found elsewhere.

Second, the typical Las Vegas game is dealt from a standard (52-card) deck. While four decks, or sometimes two decks, shuffled together are often used, the single deck is still most common. Outside Nevada the multiple-deck game predominates, and in many areas nothing else can be found.

It is far easier to learn the Archer Method under the conditions of the single-deck game. Also, under ideal circumstances, winning is easier with a single deck. Therefore, *the system described in Chapters 2 through 9 assumes a single deck.* It is not suitable for multiple decks without the adaptation given in Chapter 11. Eventually you should learn this adaptation; the multiple-deck game is entirely acceptable to play and can even be preferable under some circumstances.

In northern Nevada (the Reno-Lake Tahoe area) multiple decks are rarely seen. However, all but a few casinos there forbid certain optional tactics by the player, which will be discussed. Accordingly, the system in this book is oriented to the Las Vegas rules but in such a way that no problem occurs in adapting to Reno-Tahoe rules.

General Features

Each Twenty-One table has a dealer, a casino employee who deals the game and serves as banker, collecting and paying the players' bets.

The usual table has places for six players, although many accommodate seven. All places need not be filled; the game can proceed with only one player and the dealer.

The table is shaped approximately like a half moon. The dealer stands at the flat side; the players sit around the curved side facing him. Figure 1 shows a diagram of a six-place Twenty-One table.

The deck is shuffled by the dealer and cut by a player, and ordinarily the dealer "burns" the top card (places it face up on the bottom of the deck). As an alternative, a joker is sometimes placed face up on the bottom. This burn card is never dealt, and no joker is ever used in the cards that are dealt.

Each player places a bet, and the deal begins, clockwise. Each player is dealt two cards face down, one at a time in rotation. The dealer also gives himself two cards, the first face up and the other face down. Play then proceeds.

All players compete against the dealer—not against each other. The tactic of playing a hand is to try to make a total as close as possible to 21 without exceeding 21.

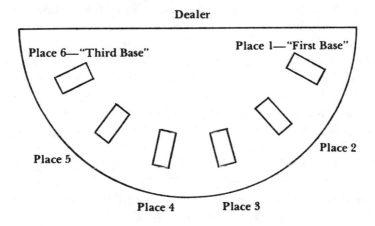

Figure 1. Six-Place Twenty-One Table (Schematic)

The value of each card is as follows:

> Each face card (K, Q, or J) counts 10.
> A pip 10 counts 10.
> Except for the Ace, all other cards (2, 3, 4, 5, 6, 7, 8, 9) count face value.
> The Ace is treated specially; it may count either as 1 or 11, as the player desires.

If a player's initial two cards consist specifically of an Ace and any card counting 10, he has a "natural," usually called a "blackjack." This hand wins immediately, and the player is paid 1½ times his bet. Similarly, if the dealer has a blackjack, the players lose immediately, although they are not required to pay off at 1½ times their bets. If both a player and the dealer have blackjack, a tie results and no money changes hands.

Except when a blackjack is involved, each player, in turn, has the option of drawing additional cards, one at a time, until he is satisfied with his hand. But if he draws and exceeds 21, he automatically loses; he has what is called a broken hand, or a "bust." The dealer draws last, if he draws at all. If he draws and breaks, he pays all players who still have a hand (all who have not broken).

If the dealer does not break, he compares his hand with that of each player who has not broken. A player's hand wins if it is higher (closer to 21) than the dealer's hand and loses if it is lower. A tie is a standoff; it neither wins nor loses. (This latter feature of the casino game is a pleasant surprise to many newcomers who are familiar only with amateur games in which the dealer wins ties.)

Except for a blackjack, the payoff is at even money—the amount of the original bet.

Drawing and Standing by the Player

If the player is satisfied with his hand on the initial two cards, he merely slides his cards face down under his bet. Such verbal terms as "I'm good" or "I stand" are generally not used in the casinos. However, a player often will exercise his option to draw additional cards to his original two in an effort to improve the hand. Detailed discussion of the best strategy for drawing will be postponed until later chapters. But as an illustration, suppose a hand consists of 4,3, for a total of 7. Obviously a card should be drawn, as no single additional card can possibly break the hand.

To draw a card, a player simply scratches his cards across the felt tabletop toward himself. Such verbal requests as "Hit me," commonly used in amateur games to ask for cards, are generally not used in casinos.

In the example given, suppose the player hits (draws to) his 4,3 and receives another 3. He now has 10 and should hit again. Suppose this time he draws a 9. He then has a total of 19 and should "stand," draw no more cards. He has a fairly good hand, and it would be foolhardy to draw more cards in an effort for further improvement. Anything but an Ace or 2 would break the hand.

When satisfied with his total, the player slides his original two cards (his hole cards) face down under his bet. He should do this without lifting the chips with his free hand. It is generally improper for the player to handle his bet unnecessarily after the deal has begun.

Suppose a player is dealt a 10,5, for a 15 total, elects to draw, and receives a 7 or higher card. The hand is now broken, and the player should turn all his cards face up immediately. The dealer will then collect the bet and move on to the next player.

It should be recalled that the Ace has an optional value of 1 or 11. In blackjack it is, of course, counted as 11. Thus, the combination of 11 and 10 counts 21. As with a broken hand, a blackjack should be turned face up immediately (and obviously with more relish).

In other hands, the ambiguous value of the Ace frequently permits advantageous maneuvering in play of the hand. For example, suppose a hand contains Ace,6. Counting the Ace as 11, this hand would total 17. But counting it as 1, the hand would total 7. The hand is known technically as a *soft* 17. And we shall see eventually that 17 is not a very good hand. Thus, the player may choose, temporarily at least, to treat the hand as a 7 and draw. He may be so fortunate as to draw, say, a 4. In this case, he would reassess the value of the Ace as 11, since 11,6,4 totals 21, the best possible hand other than a blackjack. (Note that 21 is not blackjack unless it is made up by the original two cards.)

On the other hand, when the player draws to his Ace,6, suppose he draws a 10. Clearly, he would now continue to treat the Ace as 1. The total is 1,6,10, or *hard* 17. ("Soft 27" would be out of the question, as 27 is a broken hand.)

As another example, suppose Ace,6 (soft 17) is hit, and another Ace is drawn. In this case, one Ace may be counted as 11 and the other as 1. Thus, the hand is a soft 18 (11,1,6). And through the nature of "soft" hands, soft 18 may also be treated as 8 (1,1,6). At his option, the player may stand with his 18 or may draw again. He *cannot* break. He may improve. Of course, he may also make a worse hand by drawing something like a 7 for 1,1,6,7, or "hard" 15. So a gamble is involved. In later chapters, we will consider in detail the circumstances in which soft hands and hard hands should be hit and when they should not. The decision often will be made on the basis of the value of the dealer's up-card.

It should be noted that, except for blackjacks, all two-card hands containing an Ace are "soft." That is, they have an optional value, and they cannot break. But hands of more than two cards *may* contain an Ace and not be soft. For example Ace,4,7 is *hard* 12. The Ace no longer has an optional value; it must be counted as 1 because counting it 11 would give the hand a value of 22, which is a bust. All hands not containing an Ace are "hard." Thus, 3,2 is hard 5. But if 3,2 is hit, and an Ace is drawn, the hand becomes a soft 16, with an optional value of 6.

Drawing and Standing by the Dealer

After all players have had their opportunities to draw cards, it is the dealer's turn. Unlike the players, however, his decision to draw or stand is not at his option but is dictated by the rules of the casino.

The dealer turns up his hole card. If his total is 16 or less, he *must* draw and must continue to draw until he has 17 or more. If his total is 17 or more, or when it reaches that total by drawing, he must stand. If he breaks, of course, he pays all players who have not previously done so.

The dealer also does not have the option of assigning an ambiguous value to his soft hands. For example, Ace, 7, or soft 18, must be counted as 18; it may not be regarded as an 8 and drawn to.

However, soft 17 (Ace,6) does require special mention, as casinos vary in how they treat it. By traditional rules, soft 17 is *17*, period, and the dealer must stand. But many casinos have introduced a variation in which the dealer hits soft 17. He still does not have an option; where the "soft-17 rule" is played, the dealer may not choose to stand with soft 17, but *must* draw. Needless to say, the rule does not apply to hard 17, such as 10,7 or 10,6,Ace; the dealer stands on these hands. But he hits hands such as Ace,6, Ace,4,2, and Ace,Ace,3,2.

Many casino dealers believe that the soft-17 rule improves the player's chances to win, and they sometimes volunteer this information to the players. I have no doubt of their sincerity, but they are essentially wrong. It is true that the soft-17 rule may help certain weak players, depending on just what type of unsound practices they employ. It does lead the dealer to break more often than when the traditional rule is followed. But it also allows him to make more good hands. Against good play, the soft-17 rule operates overall to the player's slight disadvantage.

Doubling Down

After receiving his initial two cards, the player may, if he wishes, double his bet and draw one card. If he elects this option, he receives *only* one card. And of course, he may not double the bet unless he is prepared to draw this one card.

To double down, the player, simultaneously with adding the extra chips to the initial bet, turns his two cards face up in front of the bet. The dealer will give the player the one additional card face down.

In northern Nevada all but a few casinos permit the player to double down only on totals of 10 and 11. The Las Vegas casinos permit doubling on any initial two cards. Restrictions on a player's options slightly reduce his chances for winning, particularly if he is an expert player of the type this book will attempt to develop. Traditionally, many casinos that restrict doubling to certain totals have largely compensated by allowing the doubling to be made with hands of three or more cards. Unfortunately, however, this option has generally been discontinued.

Splitting Pairs

When the player's first two cards consist of a numerically identical pair, such as two 8s or two 3s, another optional play is available. The player may place another bet equal to the first, turn the cards face up and separate them in front of the bets, and treat each as the first card to a new hand. He will receive another card face up on each and will proceed to play the two new hands separately.

There are, however, a few differences in how these hands are played in comparison with ordinary hands. Some casinos permit doubling down with either or both of these new hands, but most do not. Usually, if another pair is obtained after the original pair is split, the player may split again, thus making a third hand. However, a few casinos do not permit resplitting.

Aces in particular receive special treatment when they are split. Only a single card is allowed on each one; the hands cannot be hit or doubled. If a 10 or face card is drawn, the hand is not considered a blackjack, but just an ordinary 21. In the past some casinos would permit resplitting if a third Ace were drawn, but practically none will allow this any longer.

The last restriction recalls a personal experience on the Las Vegas Strip when I split a pair of Aces and received not one but *both* of the other two Aces. I could not resplit them, and thus I possessed two miserable soft 12s, which could not be hit. While the chance of such a thing happening is extremely remote, less than one in a quarter million, it did happen to me. Naturally, at that moment, I wished I were playing in one of those casinos that permitted resplitting of Aces.

Despite the various restrictions involved when Aces are split, it is usually much to the player's advantage to split them. Whether other pairs should be split depends on the dealer's up-card. Detailed discussion of when pairs should be split appears in later chapters.

Except when Aces are involved, the actual mechanics of playing the hands after a pair is split are different from those with other hands. Recall that ordinarily to draw the player scratches his cards across the table; to stand he slides them under his bet. After a pair is split, however, all the player's cards are face up; there is no need even to touch them. To draw a card he simply taps the table once behind the cards with his forefinger. To stand he waves his hand horizontally over the cards. If doubling down is allowed after splitting, the player merely adds the correct amount to the bet. No explanation is necessary; the dealer will understand that the player is doubling down and will give him one more card (customarily dealt face down).

From the previous discussion of drawing and standing by the dealer, it becomes obvious that the player should have no concern about whether his cards are seen by the dealer. (In some multiple-deck games, in fact, *all* players' hands are dealt face up.) The dealer cannot vary his play on the basis of the players' hands. Insofar as play of the cards is concerned, the dealer could just as well be a robot, but a robot could not entertain the players with friendly conversation.

The Insurance Bet

Many casinos, including virtually all in and around Las Vegas, allow a side bet that is offered whenever the dealer's up-card is an Ace. In this circumstance, the chance is substantial that the dealer has a blackjack; on the average, there are 4 chances in 13 (or more precisely, 16 chances in 51) that he has a 10 or face card in the hole. Thus, before looking at the hole card, the dealer will ask which players, if any, wish to make an insurance bet. The player taking insurance makes an additional bet equaling half his original bet. Then, if the dealer does have a blackjack, he pays the insurance bet at the rate of 2 to 1. Of course, the player loses his original bet to the blackjack (unless he also has a blackjack). Therefore, the loss of the original bet exactly pays the insurance bet, and no money actually changes hands. If the dealer does not have a blackjack, the player loses the insurance bet and play continues. The original bet then will be settled after the draw in the usual manner.

Ordinarily insurance is a bad bet. The player receives only 2 to 1 on a 9 to 4 proposition. But as we shall see in Chapter 6, it sometimes is a very good bet if a player becomes sufficiently expert to recognize precisely when it should be made. Most habitual players *think* they know when to "take insurance," but few understand the *proper* concept of sound insurance betting.

Surrender

Several years ago a new rule was introduced in the casinos of southeastern Asia, and several Nevada casinos recently have adopted a variation of it. The rule is appropriately titled *surrender*. It allows the player, at his turn to draw, to abandon his hand, give up half his bet, and retain the other half.

To employ the option the player turns his cards up in front of his bet and announces, "Surrender," or "Half." The dealer will gather in the cards and half the bet and move on to the next player. Naturally, surrender is not allowed if the dealer has blackjack. (Until the dealer has checked for blackjack, the player has no turn to draw and consequently no opportunity to surrender.) For some vague reason the classical rule did not allow surrender if the dealer's up-card was an Ace, even though the Ace did not make up part of a blackjack. Otherwise, however, the option was allowed after any number of cards were drawn, provided the hand had not broken. As played in Nevada, surrender is permitted regardless of the dealer's up-card but only if the player has not drawn any cards to his initial two.

It is surprising that more casinos have not adopted the surrender rule: by my observations, it clearly increases the casino's rate of winning. Although most players ignore the option, those who avail themselves of it almost invariably become intrigued by it and surrender far too often. However, an expert who *knows* when to opt for surrender and when to decline can use the rule to substantial advantage. The strategy for judicious surrender is given in later chapters of this book.

The Bet

Betting is ordinarily done with chips instead of cash. The dealer sells the chips to the players. The casino cashier redeems them.

All tables have a minimum and maximum limit that may be bet on a hand. One dollar is a rather common minimum, but some casinos allow less. Some tables have a $5 minimum, and occasionally a casino will have one or two tables with an even higher minimum. A common maximum limit is $500. Some casinos have a lower maximum, such as $200, and a rare one may allow as much as $1,000.

The Shuffle

The dealer may shuffle at any time between hands, but ordinarily, if enough cards remain in the deck to deal another round of hands, he will deal from this remaining portion.

Depending on the dealer and the custom of the casino, sometimes he will begin dealing a round even though few cards remain. When the deck becomes exhausted during the deal or round of drawing, he will shuffle the discards from the preceding play and continue the round. The deck is exhausted when the last card is reached. The last card is not dealt but is shuffled with the other discards.

In most Las Vegas casinos cards that have been played are retired by the dealer to a small half-box called a *return tray*. Elsewhere the dealer may place the discards face up underneath the undealt cards.

If the deck were shuffled after every deal, the expert player would be unable to gain any substantial advantage over the casino. This advantage derives his from knowledge of the cards that remain in a partially depleted deck and from his use of this knowledge to vary his betting and play. Fortunately, it is impractical for a dealer to shuffle routinely after every hand. For one thing, players simply would not remain at a table where the dealer spent half the time shuffling.

Of course, if all or even most players were experts, the casinos would have to resort to the practice of never dealing from a partially depleted deck—or else abandon the game. But only a tiny fraction of Twenty-One players are experts. A larger minority play rather well, but even these are unable to keep track of the cards that have been played and to make use of the knowledge. The great majority of players are downright incompetent, and most of them will remain so because they do not make the effort to learn and employ the methods described. But to those readers who would like the immense pleasure and satisfaction of knowing they can walk into a casino and win at this fascinating game, read on.

2

The Basic (Neutral) Strategy

THE strategy for Twenty-One developed by Baldwin and colleagues[1] and confirmed with minor variations by Thorp,[6] Jacoby,[12] Wilson,[7] Epstein,[8] Einstein,[10] Revere,[9] and others provides the proper play with an undepleted 52-card deck. It assumes a full, unaltered composition of the deck at every moment. While it is the correct strategy on the average, it is not the ideal strategy when normal fluctuation in composition of the deck occurs as cards are played and removed from the deck. However, it does provide a *basic* strategy, to be used by players who do not count cards.

But even players who do count cards will find many occasions when the deck has an approximately "average" composition. It will obviously be average when freshly shuffled and the first hand is yet to be dealt. As cards are played, the composition will fluctuate about that average.

As we shall see later, we make certain changes in play when, with the method of counting we will adopt, the

14

deck contains an abnormal ratio of 10s to other cards. When this ratio is higher than usual, we will make changes that are quite different from the changes when it is lower.

But before we can discuss changes, we must have a basic procedure. The basic strategy presented in this chapter provides that starting point. It will be played when the deck is approximately average in the ratio of 10s and face cards to other cards. (Throughout the remainder of the book, I will often mention 10s, and by that I really mean pip 10s *or* face cards.)

We shall see that when an unusually large number of 10s remain in the deck still to be played, we have an advantage and will make appropriate adjustments in the way we play and bet. When the number is unusually small, we are at a disadvantage, but we will make adjustments to minimize the disadvantage. And when the number is about average, our chances of winning or losing are about even because the situation is approximately neutral. It is also in this situation that the basic strategy is suitable. For the card-counting player, the basic strategy might better be called the *neutral* strategy.

The basic strategy I will present varies slightly from any other thus far published. I aim to provide the most convenient and suitable technique of play with a neutral deck in view of the changes to be made as the composition of the deck varies. A few of my modifications represent minor improvements over certain other strategies, and a few represent trivial compromises with theoretically ideal play. I can assure you, however, that the total effect of the innovation on winning and losing is most insignificant. The really important reason for the design of the strategy is the facility of learning and using it with the other features of my system.

When casino rules are sufficiently liberal, the player using neutral or basic strategy has a very modest advantage, even without the refinements of card counting and variations of bets and strategy. Casinos can invoke any of several rules that slightly diminish the player's chance of winning. (These variations will be discussed in Chapter 10.) But unless the variations are multiple and severe, playing basic strategy still provides practically an even bet.

The Player's Options

It will be remembered that after the player places his bet, he is dealt a hand consisting of two hole cards, and the dealer gives himself a hand of one hole card and one up-card. The player now has certain options on how to play the hand unless he has a blackjack, which is an automatic winner. If he has a pair, he must decide whether to split. He must decide whether to double down. And if he does not double down, he must decide whether to draw or stand. (If surrender is allowed, he must also decide whether to play out the hand at all.)

These decisions often are based not only on the hand itself but also on the dealer's up-card. For the advanced player they are also based in part on the other cards he has seen played. One additional decision must be considered if the dealer's up-card is an Ace—that is, whether to take insurance. But at the present stage of our discussion, this decision is ready-made. *Do not take insurance.* It is a bad bet.

It would be logical to consider the player's options in the order he decides them: first, whether to split a pair if he has one; second, whether to double down; and third, whether to stand or draw. But usually no pair is held, and

usually the hand is not one that merits any serious consideration of doubling. Thus, with the substantial majority of
hands, the real decision involved is whether to draw or
stand. Accordingly, the basic strategy for drawing or standing is presented first.

Standing or Drawing—Hard Hands

It should be remembered that a hard hand is one that
does not contain an Ace—or if it does, the total is such
that the Ace must be counted as 1 (counting it 11 would
give a total higher than 21).

Obviously, any hard hand of less than 12 must be hit
(drawn to). It cannot break. And it cannot win unless the
dealer breaks. A card should always be drawn to such a
hand in an effort to improve it.

A hand of hard 17 or above must not be hit. Any chance
of improvement is more than offset by the danger of
breaking.

Thus, the only decisions that present any problem involve
hands of 12 through 16. When they are hit, the danger of
breaking exists. But if they are not hit, they cannot win
unless the dealer breaks. Remember, the dealer never
stands unless he has a total of at least 17.

In the jargon of the game, hands of 12 through 16 are
known as "stiffs." Actually, the term *stiff* could be applied
to any hand that can break. But for practical purposes, it
is restricted to 12 through 16, since higher stiffs are not
hit.

The rules for hitting a stiff are simple:

> If the dealer's up-card is high (7,8,9,10, or Ace), a
> stiff should be hit.

> If the dealer's up-card is low (2 through 6), a stiff should not be hit—*with this exception*: hit 12 if the dealer shows a 2 or 3.

That is all there is to it, yet most Twenty-One players do not know this simple, fundamental strategy for drawing and standing with hard hands. The validity of the strategy has been confirmed repeatedly by mathematical calculations. Simple reasoning helps to understand the good sense of the strategy. If the dealer has a 7 or higher card, his chance of breaking is relatively small. There is a strong chance that he has a 10 or face card in the hole. In this case, his hand is already made, and he will not have to draw. We should, therefore, take the risk of breaking and draw to a stiff, hoping to beat the dealer's hand.

But if the dealer has a 6 or lower card, he will have to draw (unless he holds 6, Ace where the soft-17 rule is not in effect). The chances are excellent that the dealer has a 10 or some other high card in the hole. In this case, *he* must hit a stiff. The player's chances of winning are better if he lets the dealer hit his probable stiff than if the player hits his own stiff. In other words, let the dealer be the one who breaks.

The strategy of standing with a stiff against a dealer's low card greatly diminishes the one fundamental disadvantage the player has under the rules of Twenty-One. That disadvantage is the requirement that the player draw first and thus risk breaking first. It should be noted that if a particular player and the dealer both break, there is no tie, because the player has broken first and has already lost his money. Once the player breaks, he is *through*.

This disadvantage to the player is so important that he can be given the advantage of every other difference between his play and that of the dealer. The player has an option of drawing or standing and can base his decision on seeing one of the dealer's cards; the dealer has no such option. The player can double down if he wishes; the dealer cannot. The player can split a pair; the dealer cannot. And the player receives a bonus payoff for a blackjack; the dealer does not.

But if the player is handicapped (and he is) by the necessity to draw first, he can greatly compensate by following the proper strategy just given. The single exception to the principle of standing with a stiff against a low card involves the borderline advantage of hitting the 12 against a 2 or 3. But since this is the only exception, learning it should present no great problem. (To avoid any confusion, I will point out again that the player *does* stand with 12 against 4, 5, or 6.)

A visual aid to learning the basic strategy for standing or drawing to hard hands is given in Figure 2 (page 23).

Standing or Drawing—Soft Hands

The strategy for drawing or standing with soft hands is the simplest in the game. Remember that a soft hand contains an Ace and cannot break. Eg, Ace,7 is soft 18. Since soft 18 is also (optionally) an 8, no card can break it.

The strategy is as follows:

Always* hit soft 17 or less, regardless of the dealer's up-card.

Stand on soft 18 unless the dealer shows a 9 or 10.

---

*Such terms as *always* and *never* occur frequently in this book, but they must be read in context. In actuality, we often *double down* on soft 17 (and various other soft hands). But this strategy is presented later; at the moment we are discussing only standing and drawing. Even so, doubling down may be regarded as a modified form of drawing. One thing is certain: we never *stand* on soft 17—this time the word *never* is used with its unequivocal meaning.

Hit soft 18 if the dealer does show a 9 or 10.

Always stand on soft 19 and above.

What could be simpler? If the strategy seems difficult at all, figure 2 presents it in an even easier fashion.

You may wonder why, if we hit soft 18 against 9 or 10, we stand against an Ace. The decision is really very close. When the dealer has 9 or 10, we fear a 10 in the hole, and 19 or 20 will beat 18. But if the dealer's up card is an Ace, he cannot also have a 10, as then he would have blackjack and would already have collected the money.

Despite the simplicity of the strategy for drawing or standing with soft hands, it does seem to bother beginners more than the play of hard hands. I think there are two reasons. First, soft hands occur less frequently than hard hands, and there is, therefore, less opportunity to become familiar with them. Second, inexperienced players often have trouble with the ambiguous value of an Ace, which counts either 1 or 11.* Both problems are related, and the solutions are merely a bit of practice at playing.

At this point, I suggest that unless you are experienced at playing Twenty-One, you begin to deal some hands to yourself and practice the strategy for drawing or standing —temporarily ignoring the possibilities for doubling down and splitting pairs. If possible, have a friend deal to you.

But even without practice, if you have read the preceding portions of this book with care, you will be astonished by the blunders that habitual but unskilled players make daily in the play of soft hands. Many of these people have

---

* The real difficulty occurs when extra Aces are held. Accept this hint: first count each Ace as *one*, which gives the hard value, and then add *ten* a single time to this total for the soft value. For example, 3,2,A,A,A is "hard 8"; 8 + 10 = soft 18.

learned to play hard hands reasonably well. But thinking that 18 is a good hand, they consider it foolish to draw to soft 18. They forget that *soft* 18 is also an 8. And they do not seem to realize that 18 is a very poor hand when the dealer shows 9 or 10. They fear ruining their precious 18 by drawing a 9, 8, or some other bad card. They seem unable to understand that if the dealer beats them by one point, it might as well be by seven or eight; they lose their bet either way. They fail to realize that the deck contains three Aces, four 2s, and four 3s that could improve their hand and fifteen or sixteen 10s that would not hurt it.

Of course, soft 18 does represent an acceptable hand against an 8 (a potential tie), and a quite desirable hand against a 7. Accordingly, it should not be toyed with against such cards.

But soft 17 is a different matter. A 17 is a poor hand. It will beat nothing except a bust. It will tie if the dealer happens also to make 17, but otherwise it might as well be 16 or 12. So why would any sensible person ever stand on a *soft* 17, which is also a 7, when a draw has a real possibility of improving the hand, only a trivial possibility of hurting it, and no possibility of breaking it?

Yet often I have actually seen people stand with something like soft 16. They stood on a 6!

Doubling Down—Hard Hands

Doubling down with hard hands is also quite easy to learn. In basic strategy, consideration need be given only to three totals: 11, 10, and 9.

Please remember that doubling down is permitted only with two cards. Practically no casino in Nevada will any longer permit doubling after cards have been drawn to a hand. Thus, if a hand has already been hit, you must

merely continue according to the proper strategy for drawing, even though your total has reached one that ordinarily
you would want to double with.

In basic strategy, double down with hard hands as
follows:

> Always double with 11, regardless of the dealer's
> up-card.
> Double with 10 if the dealer shows 2 through 9. Do not
> double with 10 against 10 or Ace.
> Double with 9 against 2 through 6, but not against
> higher cards.

Figure 2 summarizes the basic strategy for doubling down
with hard hands.

In view of my previous captious comments, it may seem
that I have a grudge against unskilled players. But not
so—they are the ones who keep the game going. They
provide the profits to the casinos and make it possible for
experts to win.

With this explanation, then, I will discuss the common
errors made by inept players in doubling down. Some
novices, not knowing when to double, simply do not do
so at all, but most players do routinely double with 11.
Thus, even the weak players tend to be correct for a
change. However, these players also double with 10 regardless of the dealer's up-card. In doing so, they are generally
wrong when the dealer shows a 10 or Ace. Certain other
players will double with 10 or 11 only against a relatively
low card, such as 2 through 8.

Many weak players do not double with 9 at all. Those
who do so are likely to double compulsively or capriciously.
If you see a player double down with an 8, he is either a

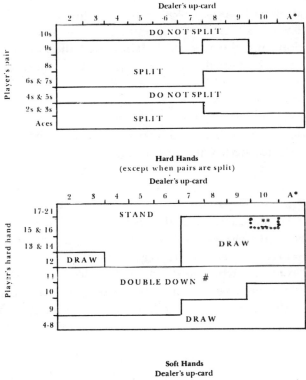

Pairs
Dealer's up-card

Hard Hands
(except when pairs are split)
Dealer's up-card

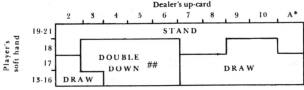

Soft Hands
Dealer's up-card

*In basic strategy, do not take insurance.
**Surrender if allowed; otherwise draw.
 # Draw if rules forbid doubling down.
Except with soft 18, draw if rules forbid doubling down; stand with
    soft 18.

Figure 2. The Basic (Neutral) Strategy

very good player (maybe an expert) or a fool. A bit of
observation will soon reveal which. Experts *know* when to
double with 8. At the moment, the less said the better
about doubling down with 8. I have not included it in the
basic strategy, but it will be discussed in later chapters.

Doubling Down—Soft Hands

The strategy for doubling down with soft hands should
be little more difficult to learn than the other strategies
previously learned. Only one broad pattern must be memorized; then two minor additions should be superimposed.

Nevertheless, the strategy *is* more difficult than the
preceding, for a single reason: it introduces a surprising
method of play that must do violence to all prejudices that
have been developed through learning the material thus
far presented in the basic strategy.

For example, who would dream of doubling down with
a terrible hand like a 6 or a 16? Ordinarily, the answer is:
no one. But a *soft* 16 is neither a 6 nor a 16. It is both or
either. And we *do* double down with soft 16 when the
dealer's up-card is 4, 5, or 6!

Before examining the logic of the strategy for doubling
down with soft hands, I will first present the strategy. It is
simple and should be memorized.

Double with soft 13 through 18 if the dealer's up-card
is 4, 5, or 6.
Double with soft 17 or 18 if the dealer's up-card is 3.

If a Twenty-One player had nothing to learn but the
soft-doubling strategy, he could master it within a few
minutes. But good play requires a knowledge of many
procedures, and all must be followed almost instinctively.

Learning to play the soft-doubling strategy is made easier by understanding why we do certain things.

Consider the soft 17, with which we double against 3 through 6. First remember that we would never *stand* with soft 17. And a bit of reflection will reveal that once we have drawn one card to it, we would never draw a second against a 3 through 6. For example, a 10 would make *hard* 17, and we do not draw to that. A 5 through 9 would make a stiff, and against low cards we generally do not draw to that. An Ace would make soft 18, and against low cards we do not draw to that. And finally, we may draw a 2, 3, or 4, for soft 19, 20, or 21, any of which we would be pleased to have. Thus, the fact that doubling down restricts the draw to only one card deprives us of nothing in the case of soft 17, as we would draw only one card against 3 through 6 in any event.* Since the dealer with one of these low cards has a fine chance of breaking, the danger of our making a poor hand is largely improved. And as noted, even if he does not break, there are several fine cards (Ace, 2, 3, or 4) that may give us a hand that will beat him anyway. Mathematics has shown that we have an advantage over the dealer when we have soft 17, he has a 3 through 6, and we draw one card. Having this advantage, we are pleased to accept the opportunity to double our bet.

Soft 18 presents a slightly different picture. The soft-

---

* The careful reader may detect an apparent exception to the statement that we would never draw but one card to soft 17 against 3: a 5 would convert the hand to hard 12, and we have learned to draw to this against 3. In later chapters, however, we will see that the very cards required to make up this particular 12 will change the composition of the remaining deck enough that we should depart from basic strategy and not draw. If this footnote seems complicated at the moment, do not let it confuse you; later chapters will make it simple.

standing strategy (pages 19-21) indicates that we stand with this hand against low cards, and the strategy is sound. But if we have our soft 18 on the first two cards, and thus have the privilege of doubling our bet and drawing one card, it is well to do so when the dealer has 3, 4, 5, or 6. The rest of the reasoning is similar to that discussed for soft 17.

In doubling down with soft 16 against 4, 5, or 6, we do face the slight possibility of drawing an Ace and thus being deprived of the opportunity to draw another card. (Remember, we always draw to soft 17 if possible.) But this slight disadvantage is more than offset by the fine chance of making an 18 through 21. Once again, if we are unfortunate and draw a high card to make a stiff, remember that we would not draw again against 4, 5, or 6 even if we could. We know from mathematics that we have an advantage with a soft 16 when the dealer has 4, 5, or 6, and we should press this advantage by doubling down.

The doubling-down strategy with soft 13, 14, and 15 involves similar reasoning. No doubling-down strategy is presented for soft 12, because the only way soft 12 is possible with two cards is to hold Ace,Ace. We shall soon learn that we *split* Aces.

In basic strategy, we do not double down with soft 19 or above. We have a probable winner already and should not toy with the hand.

It should be noticed that all soft doubling is done when the dealer shows a low card. Thus the possibilities of improving a relatively poor hand are combined with the good chance that the dealer will break.

As in the hard-doubling strategy, if casino rules forbid doubling (e.g., if you have already drawn and hold more than two cards), merely follow the strategy for drawing or standing.

A visual aid to the soft-doubling strategy is presented in figure 2.

Splitting Pairs

The proper splitting of pairs is slightly more difficult to learn than the other components of basic strategy, mostly because of the absence of the compact patterns that exist with the others. Nevertheless, if we first learn the easy management of five of the ten possible types of pairs, a pattern does emerge for four of the other five. That leaves only one to memorize individually.

The following is easy:

> Always split Aces and 8s.
> Never split 10s, 5s, or 4s.

Since 10s represent any combination of 10s, Js, Qs, or Ks, the preceding instructions embrace 8/13s of all possible pairs. There remains only to learn when to split 2s, 3s, 6s, 7s, and 9s:

> Split 2s, 3s, 6s, and 7s against 2 through 7 but not against other cards.
> Split 9s against 2 through 6 *and* against 8 and 9 (i.e., against all cards except 7, 10, and Ace).

As usual, a visual aid is given in figure 2.

Do not be confused by apparent contradictions between the strategies for splitting pairs and for drawing or standing. As an example, you now know to hit 12 against 2 but to split 6s against 2. Naturally, you cannot do both. In all circumstances like this, the pair-splitting strategy takes precedence: split the 6s; draw to other 12s.

The reasons for splitting pairs should be understood.

Aces are split for two reasons: first, a soft 12 is not a particularly attractive hand; second, two *new* hands, each starting with an Ace, present a very favorable prospect. Even though the casino rules permit only one additional card for each hand when Aces are split (see Chapter 1), the odds favor the split, regardless of the dealer's up-card.

However, the splitting of pairs is often done not so much from a wish to have two new hands but to break up a bad hand in an effort to improve the overall prospects for a win. Consider pairs of 2s, 3s, 6s, and 7s: a 4, 6, hard 12, and hard 14 are poor hands. With these hands and when the dealer shows a relatively low card, it is better to split, even at the expense of doubling the bet, and try to make at least one good hand, all the time hoping that you will get two good hands or that the dealer will break. If the dealer has a very high card, and thus may already have made a probable winning hand, we would not split the pairs; instead we would merely hit the 4, 6, 12, or 14 and hope for the best.

Splitting a pair of 8s may be either aggressive or defensive, depending on the dealer's up-card. Nevertheless, we always split it. In the first place, a hard 16 is about the worst possible hand. However, if the dealer has a relatively low card (7 or less), two hands starting with an 8 in each are quite desirable. If the dealer has a high card, it is better to double the bet and try to make one or two decent hands than to hit the hard 16.

The strategy for splitting 9s is interesting and logical. Against a 10 or Ace we do not split. While we will probably lose with our 18, we also would probably lose with *both* new hands starting with 9 each. Splitting 9s against a *dealer's* 9 is born of desperation, but we do it of necessity; our 18 would lose to his presumed 19, and thus we try to make *two* 19s to tie him. We split 9s against an 8 with delight; our 18 would only tie the dealer's presumed 18, but the two 19s we hope to make will beat him for a double win. Against 7 (a presumed 17), we forego the split and stand on our probably winning 18. But against lower cards, which will give the dealer a probable stiff to hit, we aggressively split the 9s; we may make two good hands or the dealer may break.

Tens are not split simply because a pair of 10s is a probably winning 20. Why break up this fine hand?

Fives are *never* split, because a pair of 5s adds up to 10, an excellent total with which to start a hand.*

A mathematical dissertation could be written on if and when a pair of 4s should be split. I will spare you such a treatise. In a later chapter I will return briefly to the matter, but I can assure you now that you could play steadily for days all over Nevada without encountering one situation in which you should split a pair of 4s. My present advice is elementary and sound: do not split 4s against anything; play this pair as you would any other total of hard 8.

Many unscientific players have a peculiar mental reaction when they are dealt a pair. They appear seized by some compulsion to split it and thus to have the happy prospect of playing an extra hand. Why they should be so eager to be beaten twice instead of once is not clear. The expert knows that intelligent pair splitting is as often as not a matter of making the best of a fundamentally bad situation.

The most pathetic of the compulsive pair splitters are those rank novices you will see who enthusiastically split 10s. This particular breed would not think of splitting say a J and a K or a K and a Q because they do not know they can. But give

---

*Occasionally, when you turn up a pair of 5s and double your bet, the dealer may not be sure whether you are doubling down or splitting. He will ask your intention before giving you a card. Naturally, you will be doubling down.

them specifically two Js or two Ks, and they will spill their chips all over the table in their excitement over an opportunity to ruin their very fine 20.

Surrender

You will recall from Chapter 1 that a few casinos permit the player who has drawn no cards to throw in his hand, surrender half his bet, and retain the other half.

Only two hands, hard 15 and hard 16, should be surrendered; and these should be surrendered *only* if the dealer's up card is a 10. Further, if the 16 consists of 8, 8, it should not be surrendered; the pair should be split as usual.

Do not be tempted into surrendering other hands until you have learned the advanced strategies dictated by the point count (see Chapter 7). Surrender is indicated only when your chance of winning the hand is less than 1 to 3 (or 1 *in* 4)—in other words, when you have less than half an even chance of winning. The great lure of the surrender rule is the unsound belief that the player should throw in a hand if he believes his chance of winning is less than even. Following such a strategy will lead to bankruptcy. I will not pursue the mathematics of the argument; I will point out only tnat less than an even chance is far different from less than *half* an even chance.

When you have hard 15 or hard 16 and the dealer shows a 10, you are normally advised to draw; with a neutral deck this is slightly better than standing. But even with drawing, you are more than three times as likely to lose than to win. Thus, surrender is the more prudent course if the option is allowed.*

A flash of insight may be gained into the theory of Twenty-

---

*One or two of the casinos that allow surrender do not openly announce the fact; ask about the rule whenever you do not know.

One strategies if you understand why you should surrender with, for example, hard 16 against 10 but not against 7. Under either circumstance you fear a 10 in the hole by the dealer. Also, you are probably going to break your hand when you draw. But you are beaten either way. Thus, you normally draw and hope for a small card and a good hand. But suppose you do draw a 3, for a total of 19, and the dealer has the presumed 10 in hole. If his up-card was 10, you still lose; if it was 7, you win. In summary, against a 7 you have better than half an even chance to win and should not surrender; against 10 you have *less* than half a chance and should do so.

Memorize the Basic Strategy

In later chapters we will take up advanced play in which we *do*, for good reason and in specific situations, depart from the basic strategy: split a pair of 10s or double down hard with hard 8 or 7 or even less! At other times we will not double with 11 or may not split a pair of Aces. We may even hit *hard* 17! We will do many things different from what we have learned in the basic strategy.

But all that must wait. To vary the play intelligently from the basic strategy, that strategy first must be known—*cold*. The player must be able to play basic strategy automatically and fast, almost by instinct. With a bit of practice, it is not difficult. But the strategy must be memorized, and playing it must be mastered.

An outline summary of basic strategy is presented at the end of this chapter, and figure 2 provides a visual aid. This strategy gives the player essentially an even chance against the dealer.

The next chapter presents a method of *winning* play for anyone who can use basic strategy. It is an easy, shorthand method of counting cards and using the information to make larger bets in favorable situations and smaller ones otherwise.

The method is a point-count system based on the ratio of 10s to small cards. In view of combined simplicity, accuracy, and effectiveness, it is the best method I have seen. It is my most important contribution to the game of Twenty-One.

Summary of Basic (Neutral) Strategy
Standing or drawing—hard hands

Stand on hard 17 or above vs. anything.
Stand on hard 12 through 16 vs. 2 through 6 with this exception: draw to 12 vs. 2 or 3.
Draw to hard 12 through 16 vs. 7, 8, 9, 10, or Ace.
Draw to less than 12 vs. anything (sometimes double down; see following).

Standing or drawing—soft hands

Stand on soft 19 or above vs. anything.
Stand on soft 18 vs. anything but 9 or 10 unless you double down; see following.
Draw to soft 18 vs. 9 or 10.
Draw to soft 17 or less vs. anything (sometimes double down; see following).

Doubling down—hard hands

Double with 11 vs. anything.
Double with 10 vs. 2 through 9 (not vs. 10 or Ace).
Double with 9 vs. 2 through 6 (not vs. 7, 8, 9, 10, or Ace).
Do not double with other hard hands.

Doubling down—soft hands

Double with soft 13 through 16 vs. 4, 5, or 6.

Double with soft 17 and 18 vs. 3, 4, 5, or 6.
Do not double with other soft hands.

Splitting pairs*

Always split Aces and 8s.
Never split 10s, 5s, or 4s.
Split 9s vs. 2 through 6 and also vs. 8 and 9 (not vs. 7, 10, or Ace).
Split 2s, 3s, 6s, and 7s vs. 2 through 7 (not vs. 8, 9, 10, or Ace).
In other words:

Aces:	split vs. anything.
10s:	do not split.
9s:	split vs. 2 through 6 and vs. 8 and 9.
8s:	split vs. anything.
7s:	split vs. 2 through 7.
6s:	split vs. 2 through 7.
5s:	do not split.
4s:	do not split.
3s:	split vs. 2 through 7.
2s:	split vs. 2 through 7.

Insurance

Do not take insurance.

Surrender*

Surrender hard 15 and hard 16 vs. 10. Do not surrender otherwise.

---

*When apparent ambiguity occurs, pair splitting takes precedence over all other strategies, and surrender takes precedence over drawing.

3

The Archer
Point-Count Method

THE basic strategy gives the player approximately an equal chance against the dealer, a remarkable circumstance in a casino game. But while an equal chance may be acceptable to the player who merely seeks the excitement and entertainment of casino gambling as a pastime, a far better prospect is that of winning. Thus, something must be added to the basic strategy to provide the player a positive advantage. In my efforts to master a winning system of playing Twenty-One without settling for a system that offered only a minor advantage, I invented a shorthand method of counting 10s and non-10s by a point-count technique.

The Archer Point-Count Method provides a way of constantly having an index to the approximate ratio of 10s to non-10s without complicated mental gymnastics. Often it provides the *exact* ratio. And it never requires any calculations beyond the mental ability to add units of one and to subtract units of two. It is an easy point-count method of playing 10-count strategy—a strategy that achieves excellent results against the casinos.

The principle of the 10-count strategy is the following. The 52-card deck contains 16 10s (10,J,Q,K) and 36 non-10s (Ace,2,3,4,5,6,7,8,9). In a full deck the ratio of 10s to non-10s is thus 16/36, or 0.444. On the average, if a greater number of 10s remain in the deck than normal, the player using basic strategy has an advantage. With an exactly normal ratio of 0.44, his chances of winning or losing are about even. With an abnormally high number of non-10s remaining, he is more likely to lose than to win on a given hand.

For example, suppose four hands have been dealt, including the dealer's, and the cards consisted of:

First hand——8,7,5
Second hand—— 10,8
Third hand——6,6,3,2
Dealer's hand——7,6,4

Of these 12 cards, only one was a 10, and 11 were non-10s (which in the future I will often abbreviate as X). Thus the undealt deck would contain 15 10s (16 - 1 = 15) and 25 non-10s (36 - 11 = 25), and the ratio would be 0.6 (15/25 = 0.6). In this circumstance the player would have a potential advantage on the next hand.

As another example, suppose the following hands have been dealt:

First hand—— 10,3,10 (bust)
Second hand—— 10,10
Third hand—— 10,Ace (blackjack!)
Dealer's hand——10,3,6

Of these ten cards, six were 10s and four were Xs (non-10s). Thus the undealt deck would contain ten 10s (16 - 6 = 10) and 32 non-10s (36 - 4 = 32), and the ratio would be about 0.3 (10/32 = 0.31). In this circumstance the player would be at a disadvantage on the next hand.

Obviously the player should make a large bet when he has an advantage (when the 10/X ratio is significantly more than 0.44), and a small one otherwise (when the ratio is below 0.44). The problem is to *know* when the ratio is favorable (when the deck is "10 rich") and when it is unfavorable ("10 poor"). It is not easy to perform the preceding type of calculations mentally during the midst of play. In the examples just given our hypothetical hands were the first ones dealt from a freshly shuffled deck. But in play, as subsequent hands are dealt from the partially depleted deck, it would be necessary not only to count the cards played at that time but to remember those played in previous hands and to add the figures together.

Some experts have mastered the technique, but the number must be small; the obvious rarity of such players is reflected by the few really good players I have observed in the many hours I have spent at the tables. One would think that if any group would be highly represented by expert players, it would be the dealers. Yet many of these people, in addition to dealing as professionals, also play as customers. I am not speaking of the shills that some casinos use to sit and play at uncrowded tables but of dealers who play with their own money during their free time. And most of these individuals do not play particularly well. They usually play a far better game than that of the average player, but relatively few are experts.

With sufficient persistence a person might be able to master the technique of making the rapid, continuing calculations of

10/X ratios and varying the bets and play accordingly. But when my initial efforts to do so were not encouraging, I began to look for a simpler way. It occurred to me that since only two types of cards are counted and the two counts are compared to each other in a systematic manner, it might be possible to assign some arbitrary point-count value to each type and arrive at some useful *key* to the 10/X ratio. The point-count method that I will now explain was the result.

In the past all 10-count strategies have been described by using ratios in terms of non-10s to 10s, which results in a cumbersome and confusing use of common fractions. The decimal fractions resulting from my 10/X ratios greatly simplify learning the system. The student does not even need to follow the arithmetic; he should bear in mind only that a ratio larger than 0.44 is favorable, and one below that is unfavorable. The counting system to be described coincides nicely: a high count is favorable; a low count is unfavorable. In fact, in the actual *use* of the system, I do not even ask you to remember ratios per se; instead, playing strategies are discussed in terms of point-count totals. Relating these totals to 10/X ratios helps to explain the system.

The Method

I assign a positive value of *one* to each non-10 (X) that is played. I assign a negative value of *two* to each 10. Starting with a value of *zero* before the first card is dealt from a freshly shuffled deck, I mentally add one point ("plus one") every time an X is played and subtract two points ("minus two") every time a 10 is played.

As there are 36 non-10s in a deck, it is readily seen that when all these cards are played, they would total plus 36. Similarly, the total value of 16 tens, valued at minus two each, is minus 32. Thus when all 52 cards in a deck have been played, the correct final point count must always be exactly plus 4 (36 - 32 = 4).*

Of course, if there are no more cards remaining to be played, the point count is academic. But the interesting thing is to examine the significance of a plus-4 point count when it occurs during the deal of a deck as a result of the normal chance fluctuations in the fall of the cards.

Suppose only two hands have been dealt since the shuffle, yours and the dealer's, and both happen to consist of 8,9. Four Xs will be counted (plus 1 each), and the point-count total will be plus 4. Simple arithmetic reveals that the remaining deck now contains 32 Xs and the original 16 10s. And 16/32 = 0.5, the 10/X ratio.

As another example, assume again a freshly shuffled deck from which the following hands are dealt:

First hand——10, 3, 2, 6
Second hand——9, 5, 4
Third hand——10, 10
Fourth hand——8, 7, 5
Dealer's hand——10, 4, 2, Ace

Counting these cards one at a time would proceed like this, starting with the first hand and an initial point-count total of

---

*Strict grammarians and mathematicians may challenge the adjectival uses of the terms *plus* and *minus* that I have adopted to explain this point-count method. "Plus 4," for example, might better be designated *positive 4*. Four is usually understood to be a positive quantity unless qualified otherwise. "Minus 2" might better be designated *negative 2*. But I have had to devise a nomenclature to serve two purposes: to make a technical presentation simple and to

zero: 10 (minus 2); 3 (minus 1)*; 2 (zero again); 6 (plus 1); 9 (plus 2); 5 (plus 3); 4 (plus 4); 10 (plus 2); 10 (zero); 8 (plus 1); 7 (plus 2); 5 (plus 3); 10 (plus 1); 4 (plus 2); 2 (plus 3); Ace (plus 4). Thus with these particular 16 cards played, we again have a plus-4 count. Now let us observe the effect on the remaining deck by having these cards played and thus removed. Four 10s were played, and since 16 - 4 = 12, the remaining deck contains 12 10s. Twelve Xs were played, and since 36 - 12 = 24, the remaining deck contains 24 Xs. And 12/24 = 0.5. *Again* we have a ratio of 0.5 when the point count is plus 4.

Assume that another round of hands is dealt from the deck just discussed, which has now been reduced to only 36 unplayed cards consisting of 12 10s and 24 Xs. Suppose that during this second round five more 10s and ten more Xs are played. The total negative values contained in this round would obviously be minus 10 (5 [-2] = -10), and the total positive values would be plus 10. Thus in our point-count method these five 10s exactly cancel out the ten Xs. But when this round began, remember that we already had a point count of plus 4. With 15 more cards now played, our previous 36-card deck is reduced to 21 cards consisting of 7 10s and 14 Xs. Once again we find a ratio of 10s to Xs of 0.5 (7/14 = 0.5).

It can be shown that at any stage in the play, whenever the point count is exactly plus 4, the ratio of 0.5 provides the player an advantage over the casino.

---

provide a practical mnemonic device for use in casino play. Most of us silently verbalize when keeping the point count at the tables. *Minus* has one less syllable than *negative* (and *plus* is easier to say than *positive*); thus the thought process is easier. Mistakes in play are probably reduced.

---

*The current, adjusted count is in parentheses. Thus, the pip 3, which is counted plus one, when added to the prior minus two, brings the count to minus one, as shown in the parentheses.

Whenever the point count *exceeds* plus 4, the advantage is even better, and it increases as the point count increases. It is easy to see that each time a non-10 is played, the count rises by plus 1, and the remaining deck is depleted of one more card that, with few exceptions, it is well for the player to have absent from the remaining cards to be dealt.

Suppose the initial 14 cards dealt from a full deck happen to consist of 12 Xs and only 2 10s. Since the initial count was zero, the play of these 14 cards would bring the count to plus 8, as 2 of them counted minus 2 each and 12 counted plus 1 each. The remaining deck of 38 cards contains 14 tens and 24 Xs. 14/24 = 0.58, or about 0.6. And 0.6 is a very desirable ratio for the player.

On the other hand, suppose the first 12 cards played from a full deck consist of 6 10s and 6 Xs. It is readily seen that these cards give a point-count total of minus 6. The remaining deck will contain 10 10s and 30 Xs for a ratio of about 0.3 (12/32 = 0.33). This is an unfavorable ratio for the player, and the bet should be minimal.

Any minus point count is, on the average, unfavorable. In fact, for betting purposes, you should decline to make large bets until the count reaches plus 4 or above. The reader may wonder why, if plus 4 is favorable and zero (assuming a full deck) is neutral, any plus values between zero and 4 should not be regarded at least as moderately favorable. The answer is important. Whereas we have shown that the 10/X ratio is always a favorable 0.5 when the count is plus 4, the ratio does *not* remain a neutral 0.44 when the count remains at zero as the cards are played.

If half of the deck has been played, for example, the ratio is 0.44 when the count is plus 2, not *zero*. Understand that half the deck consists of 26 cards. If the 26 cards that have been played happen to consist of exactly 8 10s and 18 Xs, the point count is plus 2. The remaining cards consist also of 8 10s and 18 Xs, and 8/18 = 0.44.

It follows that when the deck is half played, a zero point count reflects a lower ratio of 10s to Xs than when the deck is complete and thus reflects a definitely unfavorable point count. Calculations similar to the preceding will show that when the deck is one-fourth depleted, a plus-1 count reflects a neutral deck (ratio 0.44). When the deck is three-fourths depleted, a plus-3 count reflects a neutral deck. And at this latter point, of course, a plus-2 count reflects a slightly but definitely unfavorable ratio.*

We shall see eventually that for all point-count totals except plus 4, the *degree* of advantage or disadvantage will vary somewhat with the size of the unplayed deck. The smaller the unplayed deck, the greater is the advantage with any total above plus 4, and the greater is the disadvantage with any minus total. The beauty of this system is the constancy with which plus 4 reflects a small but definite advantage and thus provides the convenient point of departure at which to begin increasing the size of the bets.**

This discussion anticipates matters to be presented in later chapters. At the moment, however, it is well for the reader to remember, in a general way, the effect that depletion of the deck has upon the point-count value for a neutral deck. This effect is presented graphically in figure 3. If the matter appears complicated at the moment, return to it later.

---

*When no return tray is used for the discards, you can still estimate the degree of depletion by glancing at the side of the deck in the dealer's palm. The discarded portion, face up on the bottom, will usually have a slightly different hue from the undealt portion, and a distinct break can be seen between the two.

**Caution: the point count as presented in this chapter is not suitable for a multiple-deck game. A method of adapting it to multiple-deck games will be presented in Chapter 11.

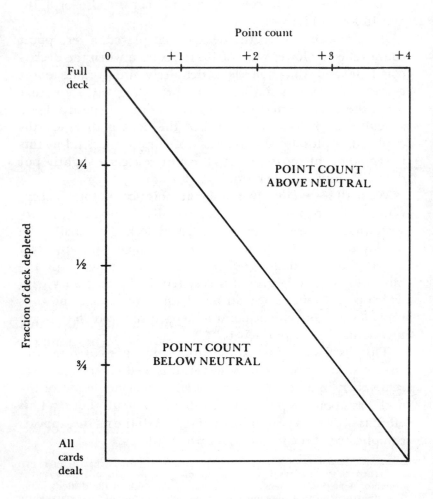

Figure 3. The Exactly Neutral Deck

If a player chooses, he *may* regard plus 3 as favorable for betting purposes early in the deck—or even plus 2 if it is very early. However, this refinement is unnecessary, particularly at this stage. The bare plus 4 does not represent an overwhelming advantage—only in the neighborhood of 1 percent. If the player has limited capital, and most of us do, he would do well to allow a slight margin of safety instead of striving to increase bets at any excuse. Any experienced gambler knows (and mathematicians have demonstrated) that even with a moderate advantage, a run of bad luck can wipe out a small bankroll.

The reader may legitimately wonder why, if plus 4 represents the constant (and favorable) ratio, I did not design the system to start with a value of minus 4, letting zero represent the constant at which higher betting starts. I could have followed that course, but in beginning to practice counting, I found a greater tendency to make mistakes during excursions through the negative values. By starting at zero, I moderately reduced the frequency of working with the negative counts. It was more comfortable to begin at zero* in beginning to count from a full deck.

In Summary

As the cards are played, start from zero and count "plus 1" for each non-10 that is seen (each Ace, 2, 3, 4, 5, 6, 7, 8, or 9).

Count "minus 2" for each 10 (10, J, Q, or K).

Add and subtract figures constantly to maintain a current point count.

Whenever the point count reaches plus 4 or anything higher than plus 4, tend to bet relatively large amounts.

---

*When I am playing and counting silently to myself, I mentally verbalize the count of zero as "even" instead of "zero." In presenting the method in this book, I usually use the term *zero*, as it is more logical: *even* might seem to connote neutrality of the count, and a zero count is neutral only when the deck is freshly shuffled. While I recognize that *even* is a slight misnomer, I am more comfortable in using it instead of the term *zero*. Perhaps the matter is pure habit. Since you are just beginning to learn the method, I do not know whether you also might find counting *even* instead of *zero* more comfortable. Just remember that *even* in this sense does not necessarily imply a neutral deck.

Whenever the point count is lower than plus 4, including any minus total, bet minimal amounts.

In general, the higher the point count, the greater the advantage to the player. Plus 4 should be regarded as the dividing line between a favorable and a nonfavorable deck.

Until you learn material in later chapters, use basic strategy in playing the hands (see Chapter 2).

Bonus: If you can grasp now *why*, with a half-depleted deck, a point count of plus 2 reflects the same 10/X ratio as zero reflects with a full deck (see figure 3), you will have a head start in understanding certain advanced refinements to be presented later.

Learning to Count

I suggest that at this point, the reader begin to practice the point-count method. Simply turn through a deck of cards, exposing them one at a time, and count each card in succession. Remember: each X is counted as plus 1, and each 10 as minus 2. Do this repeatedly until you can count the deck very rapidly without error. You will know that your final count is correct if the last card of the deck brings the point-count total to plus 4.

After you can accomplish this exercise rapidly and accurately, begin to play actual hands, using basic strategy and keeping the count as you play. If possible, get someone to deal to you, but it is reasonably satisfactory to deal to yourself if necessary.

While you learn to play hands and keep the point count, it is just as well to begin to practice the bet variation that makes the system pay off.

Bet Variation

I suggest the following for a starter. When the deal begins from a full deck, bet one unit (one chip), however you designate it. I suggest $1 for simplicity. Continue to bet one chip on each hand unless the count reaches plus 4 or above. When it does reach plus 4, bet two chips. Return to betting one chip whenever the count falls below plus 4 or whenever the deck is depleted and must be reshuffled.

Also remember that whenever the deck is exhausted in the midst of the play of a hand, the discards from previous hands are shuffled, and the deal continues from these cards to complete the play of the hand in progress. In this case, the count resumes from zero, and the subsequent count includes those cards that remain in play and those that are dealt from the newly shuffled partial deck.

With this method of practice you eventually should win a modest amount. If you fail to do so immediately, do not become discouraged; in the short run, Twenty-One is still a game of luck. The purpose of the system is to make you lucky more often than you are unlucky—in the long run. Of course, if you continue to lose with the method of practice I have suggested, you should check the accuracy of your counting and your play of the basic strategy. But do not expect miracles from this elementary method of practice. Remember that you are just starting and also keep in mind that millions of people play in casinos with no mathematical chance whatever. You *do* have a winning system.

To test the system you may wish to increase your bets *greatly* whenever the point count exceeds plus 4. Do so if you wish. If you are playing and counting properly, you will be reassured when you win, as you inevitably must.

However, for the card-counting player, the luxury of wild and precipitous changes in the size of bets is impractical in the casinos. The entrepreneurs of these luxury palaces are sensitive to the fact that a limited number of experts have the skill to beat them at Twenty-One. They don't mind too much when they lose to an occasional lucky fool; this is a hazard of the business, and the winner will probably be back to lose his bundle anyway. But they are annoyed by knowledgeable and calculating winners.

The card counter is known in the jargon of the game as a "caser," a player who can "case" the deck. If he is good, the casinos are not especially happy to have him at the tables. The dealers are instructed to use certain measures to counter his skill. (Some of these countertactics will be discussed in Chapter 10 and elsewhere.) The obvious and fundamental way to frustrate a caser, or "case-down" player, is to shuffle the deck whenever he makes a large bet, thus wiping out the 10-rich unplayed portion of the deck that remains.

Accordingly, the card-counting player must use a bit of camouflage to conceal his activities. In part, this involves making only moderate, unstartling changes in the bets. In fact, if the card counter is not too greedy, even when recognized or detected, he is usually tolerated to a degree, treated with at least normal courtesy, and sometimes shown real admiration and respect. But there is a limit to all this; the casino operators are not in business to allow expert gamblers to take away their profits. Therefore, it is expedient for the card counter to hide, as far as possible, the fact that he knows how to win. With this consideration in mind, I suggest that, after some initial practice with unrestrained bet variation, you perfect your play by practicing a realistic system of betting.

In serious play in the casinos, I often bet two chips when a full, freshly shuffled deck is to be dealt. On the next hand, I step down to one chip if the deck is not favorable. I increase to three or four chips (usually four) if the deck is favorable (plus 4 or better). Alternatively, if I start with one chip, I seldom increase to more than two the first time the deck turns favorable, reserving the four-chip bet for the subsequent hand if the deck is still favorable. Only occasionally do I bet more than four, and I reserve this luxury for the occasions when the deck is *highly* favorable. Whatever a particular bet is, I rarely increase my next bet by more than double the amount, despite the fact that the point count may suddenly have turned favorable. However, I do not hesitate to *decrease* a bet from several chips on one hand to one on the next if the count has turned unfavorable.

This strategy is explained as follows. It is very normal for a gambler to "double-up and catch-up" after a loss. It also is normal to let a winning bet "ride" in an effort to parlay the win. It is not at all unusual to win or lose a large bet and then go back to a small bet. But if a player is seen to make a series of small bets and suddenly to make a very large bet, he will be suspected of *knowing* something. As a card-counting player, of course, you *will* know something, so resist the temptation to make a large win all at once. The dealer may already suspect you of casing the deck. And if you suddenly excite him with a large bet, he will probably shuffle. Be satisfied with a moderate increase in your bet to preserve your advantage.

Some Refinements of Counting Cards

As you practice playing hands and counting cards, you undoubtedly will develop a comfortable technique of keeping the count and will discover certain shortcuts to avoid counting each card one by one. Since the play in the casinos is usually very fast, it is essential to establish some habitual routine in counting, and it is helpful to count certain commonly recurring groups of cards as units.

I have found it most expedient, as a rule, to count the cards not at the moment they are first seen but instead when they are gathered in by the dealer and the bets are settled. Recall that in all single-deck games (which is the only thing we are considering at the moment), the hole cards are face down, and thus typically not seen. When players draw cards, I ignore their up-cards temporarily unless they break. In this case, they turn up their hole cards, the dealer collects the hand, and I count all these cards, incorporating them into the point total. When a player turns up a blackjack, I do not count it until the dealer pays it and retires it to the discards. (Some dealers pay blackjacks immediately, some wait until it would be the player's turn to draw, and others wait until the final showdown, after everyone has drawn.) Except for the broken hands and blackjacks that are paid early, I delay the count until the dealer turns up his hole card and begins his draw, if any. Then, I count the dealer's hand and each player's hand as the bets are settled.

I strongly recommend this technique. If an effort is made to rush matters and count all cards at the first instant they are seen, it is very easy to become confused later, at the showdown, and count the same cards a second time or fail to count some cards at all.*

I recommend the practice of counting by groups. For example, it is readily apparent that mental steps are saved if a hand of 10,10 is simply recognized promptly as minus 4, thus avoiding the need mentally to subtract two from the preceding point total twice. Similarly, seeing a 10,5,Ace,4 should not require the involved process of subtracting two from the total and adding one three times in separate steps; a 10 and three non-10s should be recognized as a *unit* amounting to plus 1.

---

*In later chapters we shall see that at some times it *is* helpful to use all information to be gained from the cards on the table before they are finally incorporated into the count. But this matter does not apply at the moment.

For purpose of illustration, the common groupings follow. Others are possible but do not occur often, and it would be pointless to list them all. For convenience, I continue the practice of designating all non-10s (Ace, 2, 3, 4, 5, 6, 7, 8, 9) in the examples by an X.

    10,10——minus 4 (Frequent)
    10,X,10——minus 3 (Frequent broken hand)
    10,X,X,10——minus 2 (Broken hand)
    10,X,X,X,10——minus 1 (Broken hand)
    10,X——minus 1 (Very frequent)
    10,X,X——zero (Very frequent)
    10,X,X,X——plus 1
    10,X,X,X,X——plus 2
    X,X——plus 2 (Frequent)
    X,X,X——plus 3 (Frequent)
    X,X,X,X—plus 4
    X,X,X,X,X——plus 5

With experience, you will begin sometimes to group two hands together, for purposes of counting—or even more than two hands if not many cards are involved.

Pause and practice before attempting to master the following chapters. Our next presentations will involve variations in the method of play of hands, depending on the point count. But these refinements cannot be employed without the ability to play basic (neutral) strategy and to keep the accurate point count almost automatically—all the time making intelligent bet variations to take advantage of favorable point totals. When the techniques thus far presented have been thoroughly mastered, the reader will be prepared to proceed further and become a true expert at the game of Twenty-One.

A Further Advantage of the Archer Point-Count Method

Most point-count methods require the player to identify and compare more than two groups of card rankings. Often some ranks are ignored in the mental count to be remembered. But they cannot really be ignored in the process of counting itself, since they must be identified in the midst of the other cards in order to be relegated to the "uncounted" ranks. Counted ranks must similarly be identified and sorted out for their proper role in the point-count total.

One of the advantages of the Archer Point-Count Method is that it includes all cards and reduces them to only two ranks —10s and non-10s. No third group must be identified for different handling. (The separate count of Aces, to be discussed in Chapter 9, is *not* an exception to this statement. The Ace count will be superimposed upon the point count, not incorporated into it. For purposes of the point count itself, Aces will always be counted as non-10s.)

4

A Good Deck

ALTHOUGH playing basic strategy and increasing the size of bets when the point count reaches plus 4 provide a winning method, the technique does not begin to exploit the possibilities available to the expert Twenty-One player. As previously explained, it is necessary also to alter the method of play of many hands as the deck changes in composition. This is done to take advantage of favorable situations and to minimize losses in unfavorable situations.

If the human brain could function as a computer under the conditions of the casino game, an optimum method of playing every hand could be calculated rapidly. In practice, however, such finesse is not possible. The compromise, then, is to commit generalizations and approximations to memory and to call upon these data during the play of hands.

The great generalization of the 10-count methods is to treat each non-10 as equal to every other. Yet, of course, they are far from equal. In fact, while it is much to the player's

51

advantage to have, for example, a 5 out of the deck, it is to his disadvantage to have an Ace out. But overall and on the average, having non-10s out of the deck and 10s in improves the player's chances.

Within the framework of that generalization, the strategy variations for playing each hand according to the ratio of 10s to non-10s have been calculated close to exact precision. But no great loss of effectiveness occurs if, for the sake of ease in memorizing, less precise approximations are employed. This chapter and the following chapters will present strategy changes to be adopted as the point count changes by stated degrees. Chapters 6 and 7 will give progressive strategy adjustments to help you take advantage of a favorable deck. Chapter 8 will give defensive adjustments to help a player ride out an unfavorable deck with minimal losses. And Chapter 9 will present a corrective adjustment in betting strategy that minimizes the one important defect of the 10 count—the anomalous effect of Aces.

Strategy Changes at Plus 4

Whenever the point count reaches plus 4 and whenever it is at *any point higher* than plus 4, a few hands are played in a different manner from the basic (neutral) strategy. The indicated changes follow.

*Stand with hard 15 or hard 16 vs. 10.**

This variation may seem surprising. After all, with the deck 10-rich, there is even more chance than usual that the dealer has 20 and thus will beat your 15 or 16. But there is also the fact that if you *draw*, you will be even more likely than usual to break. Thus, the prospects of winning this hand

------

*The variation does not apply to 8,8. Split this pair as usual.

are somewhat dim. But a ray of hope may be found in the possibility that the dealer does *not* actually have another 10 in the hole but some small card that would give him a stiff. By the same token, there is more than a normal chance that *he* will break.

Thus, standing on your 15 or 16 vs. 10 with a relatively 10-rich deck is a defensive maneuver, executed out of necessity. You do not *want* to stand, but you should be afraid to draw. Stand and hope for the best. In the long run you will lose less often with 15 or 16 vs. 10 if you draw with the deck neutral or below (on the negative side of neutral as indicated by the point count). But you will lose less often if you stand with the deck 10-rich (as indicated by plus 4 or above).

You may wonder why, if you stand on 16 against 10 with the count at plus 4, you do not also stand against, for example, an 8. After all, if the dealer has his presumed 10 in the hole, his 18 will beat your 16 just as surely as his 20 would have.

The answer is: if you draw and do not break, you have a rather good chance of beating his presumed 18. But if you draw against his presumed 20, you may have the good fortune not to break (drawing a 3, let us say) but still lose. In other words, the overall prospects for drawing to 16 against some threatening high card other than 10 are better than drawing against a 10 itself.

In later chapters we shall find circumstances, as the point count becomes more and more favorable, in which we will be more and more inclined to stand on high stiffs against high cards. For example, at plus 8 we will stand with hard 14 vs. 10 and with hard 16 vs. 9; at plus 12 we will stand with hard 13 vs. 10, with hard 15 vs. 9 or Ace, and with hard 16 vs. Ace. But in all these circumstances the true implications of the strategy should be appreciated. In the midst of a favorable deck, we will win *most* hands, but we will sometimes draw a stiff while the dealer has drawn a high card. The decision to stand on certain of these stiffs against certain high cards is made in an effort to make the best of a bad situation.

When the surrender strategy is discussed further, we shall see that in all these dilemmas we will surrender if possible. You have already learned from Chapter 2 to surrender with hard 15 or 16 against 10 even when the deck is neutral. However, since the surrender option is usually not available, it is quite important to know when to stand with a stiff against a high card.

Stand with hard 12 vs. 2 and 3.

Thus, except for the 15 and 16 vs. 10 preceding, the hard-standing strategy really becomes simplified at plus 4; we no longer bother with drawing to 12 vs. 2 and 3.* With a 10-rich deck we would be more likely than usual to draw a 10 and break our 12. If we stand, the dealer is more likely than usual to have a 12 or 13 and to draw another 10 to break himself.

*Double down with 9** vs. 7.*

With proportionately extra 10s in the deck we have a better chance of making a 19 to beat the dealer's presumed 17. (But at plus 4, do not extend this reasoning and double with 9 vs. 8; this is statistically unsound until the count approaches plus 12, the subject of a later chapter.)

Double down with 8 vs. 5 or 6.

In this case, with a moderately 10-rich deck, we expect the dealer to break his presumed 15 or 16. (Even if he does not,

---

*Split 6,6, as usual.

**In writing of a hand of 9 or 8 or of any hand of 11 or less, I mean one without an Ace. I usually avoid such terms as "hard 9," as there is no such thing as "soft 9." If a hand that might count 9 *did* contain an Ace, I would designate it *soft 19.*

there still remains the slight chance of a win with the 18 we hope to make.)

Double down with soft 17 and soft 18 vs. 2.

Double down with soft 19 (!) vs. 5 or 6.

All this, of course, is in addition to the soft-doubling strategy presented in Chapter 2 for the neutral deck. Please recall the discussion of our reasons for doubling down with soft hands. I will not repeat it here in detail. A major factor is the strong possibility that the dealer will break, and at plus 4 he is more likely to do so when showing a low card than he is under the same circumstances when the deck is neutral. We double down with a few more soft hands at plus 4 than when the deck is neutral.

The pair-splitting strategy is unchanged at plus 4.

Summary

The changes to be made from basic strategy to take fuller advantage of a good (plus-4), 10-rich deck are summarized as follows:

Stand on hard 15 or hard 16 vs. 10 (8,8 excepted).
Stand on hard 12 vs. 2 through 6 (6,6 excepted).
Double on hard 9 vs. 2 through 7.
Double on hard 8 vs. 5 or 6.
Double on soft 19 vs. 5 or 6.
Double on soft 18 vs. 2 through 6.
Double on soft 17 vs. 2 through 6.

5

Refinements of
Card Counting

SUBSEQUENT chapters will outline various
changes to be made from the neutral strategy (and from the
plus-4 strategy just presented). These changes will be corre-
lated with the point count, which is simply an index to the
composition of the deck still to be dealt. While changes in the
size of bets (discussed in Chapter 3) must be based on the
count before any cards are dealt to the next hand, full use of
the point count for purposes of changes in *play* should be
based on every detail of information that can be gained. This
means taking the point-count value of your own hole cards
before the draw (and even during the draw), the dealer's up-
card, and all other players' cards that are seen. In other
words, for purposes of drawing, standing, doubling down, and
splitting pairs, you should adjust the point count to the *current* situation in which your decision must be made. This
counting adjustment has often been called the *running count*.
In my method, however, the term *running count* is more

applicable to the point count between completed rounds of deals from a partially depleted deck. The count that we are considering now, which we obtain during the play of a round, is more suitably called the *temporizing count*.

Before each deal, you must implant in your mind the point count at that moment (the running count) and retain it until you count other cards as they are retired to the discards. During the play of a hand, let us say you are dealt a 12 and the dealer's up-card is a 2. Your proper play, whether to draw or stand, will be based not so much upon the count before the cards were dealt but upon the count at the moment, based upon every card that can be seen. Thus, it is expedient to remember firmly one count and temporarily to consider the effect upon this count of other visible cards, purely to decide how to play the particular hand under consideration.

The practical danger of attempting to make a final count of each card at the moment it is first seen was explained in Chapter 3. It is difficult at the showdown, when all cards are turned up and taken in rapidly by the dealer, to ignore all the cards you have already counted and to add only the previously unseen cards to the count.

The following example of two rounds of hands should be enough to illustrate the use of the changing count in the midst of play. Assume that there are two players plus you at the table and that the deck has just been shuffled. Assume further that you were unable to see the card that the dealer burned. Thus the point count before the deal is zero. Then assume the dealer's up-card is a 2, you are dealt a 7,5, and the other players, who are on your right, draw a 6 and an 8, respectively. Both stand. Now it is your turn to draw.

In neutral strategy you would draw to your 12 against the dealer's 2. But now you can see 5 Xs. Since you cannot yet see the dealer's hole card or the other players' hole cards, they are ignored for the moment. Counting plus 1 for each of the cards you do see, the temporizing count is plus 5, and with plus 4 or above, you should stand with 12 vs. 2.

To continue the example, assume the dealer makes his draw and the showdown reveals the following (hole cards underlined):

First player——5,3,6
Second player——6,3,8
Your hand——7,5
Dealer——10,2,10 (Bust)

Examination will show that the count at the beginning of the next round is plus 5 (2 10s for minus 4 and 9 Xs for plus 9, to give a total of plus 5).

On the next hand you are dealt Ace,7, and the dealer's upcard is 2. At plus 4 and above you know to double down with soft 18 vs. 2. But you delay the decision until you see what the players do who must draw ahead of you. Suppose things proceed like this: the first player draws a 10 and turns up his hole cards, 10,2 showing a bust. (A good card counter would not have drawn, but he was playing correct basic strategy.) The second player draws a 10 and turns up his hole cards, 10,6 (a stupid draw under the circumstances).

Now you take rapid account. At the beginning the count was plus 5. Your Ace,7 and the dealer's 2 brought it temporarily to plus 8. But the four 10s and the two Xs reduced this count to plus 2. Thus, you do not double but simply stand with your 18.

Counting by Inference

Earlier I might have lost the reader's confidence if I had proclaimed that by the end of Chapter 5 he would be able to count cards that he could not see. It is common to find in literature on card-counting systems for Twenty-One the advice that unseen cards should be ignored. Yet to ignore hidden cards whose point-count values can logically be deduced is to waste a valuable storehouse of information. You *can* count many cards that you cannot see.

The most obvious unseen card that can be counted with confidence is the dealer's hole card when his up-card is an Ace. Clearly, if he has not turned up a blackjack and settled everything on the spot, that hole card must be a non-10; thus plus 1 can be incorporated into the temporizing point count during play of a hand. Many players' up-cards are essentially as reliable.

If a player draws a 10 and stands, his hole cards *must* be Xs or he would have broken and turned up his hand. When information is needed for the temporizing count to decide the play of a hand, any hand that has drawn only a 10 *and stands* counts zero (see the discussion of counting by groups in Chapter 3). Similarly, if a player draws a 10 and another (small) card and *stands*, his total hand in terms of point count must amount to plus 1. (He has a 10, the X you see, and the two Xs you know he must have in the hole.)

Occasionally you may be deceived by a novice who does not know that he must turn up a broken hand. The dealer will quickly instruct such a person in proper play for the purpose of future hands. Also, a player sometimes may misread his hand and stand with a bust. But these annoyances are uncommon. It is highly advantageous to count unseen hole cards, based upon what reasonably can be inferred from the up-cards that are drawn. Notice also that when a player draws such a mess of small cards as 2,3,4,4,2, he *must* have two more non-10s in the hole; you can *see* enough cards to total plus 5, but you can *infer* that the entire hand totals plus 7.

However, no reasonable inference usually can be drawn from a hand that draws a 5 or some other small card and stands. The player may either have two non-10s in the hole or one 10 and one non-10. In such cases the unseen cards should be disregarded.

Estimating by Inference

It would be possible to devise an entire additional sub-strategy of counting by inference, counting on the basis of probable hole cards as derived from the up-cards. But such a scheme would have to be adapted to the vagaries of play by the incompetents always to be found at the tables. It is risky to try to infer the value of hole cards except in obvious situations. Nevertheless, speculative inferences can be made to advantage in some circumstances.

Barring an error by the player, we *know,* for example, that the draw of a 10 implies two non-10s in the hole if the player stands. But a wealth of information is concealed by "pat" hands, hands of two hole cards on which the players stand without drawing. The question arises: can anything be known about these hands? The answer is: *not precisely.* But both from mathematics and long experience, I have found that much can be estimated: *usually* a pat hand consists of one 10 and one non-10 (minus-1 total).

Understand that any random two cards should not be assumed to consist of a 10,X. No inference should be drawn about two hole cards unless their holder gives some clue about them. But in the play of Twenty-One, a two-card hand that *stands,* drawing no cards, usually consists of 10,X.

Some such hands will, of course, be 10,10 and will thus introduce a serious error when counted as minus 1 instead of minus 4; some others will be X,X and amount to plus 2 instead of the presumed minus 1. But these errors tend to cancel one another out. It is better to be approximately right most of the time than to ignore pat hands in taking the temporizing count.

For example, imagine a freshly shuffled deck and a table with five players. You sit fifth.

First hand: pat
Second hand: ditto
Third hand: ditto
Fourth hand: ditto
Your hand: 3,4
Dealer's hand: 3 and hole card

You now draw, and the card is a 5. You have 12. You can *see* a 3, 4, 3, and 5, for a temporizing count of plus 4. According to the plus-4 strategy (Chapter 4), you should stand.

But the four pat hands, simply because they are pat, very probably contain several 10s. By the criteria I have just given for an estimated temporizing count, each is counted minus 1, and the temporizing count reverts to zero. Accordingly, you should draw.

At the showdown, the cards may well be as follows —

First hand: 10,7 (minus 1)
Second hand: 10,10 (minus 4)
Third hand: 9,8 (plus 2)
Fourth hand: 10,6 (minus 1)
Your hand: 3,4,5,5
Dealer's hand: 3,10,4

You tie instead of losing. The sample hands, of course, are invented to make a point. Had all the 10s in the hidden pat hands been ignored, you would not have dared to draw to your 12, because of the inaccurate plus-4 temporizing count. But the estimated zero count (plus 4 and minus 4 equal zero) induced you to draw your expected small card and salvage your bet. The temporizing count is a provisional count—one to be corrected when all available data are known but to be put to practical use when needed in the interim.

More on the Temporizing Count

It should be mentioned that the extra work of taking the temporizing count is not necessary on every hand. For example, suppose you are dealt hard 19. Regardless of the point count or the dealer's up-card, this is a hand on which you will stand. There is no need to bother making a temporizing count; merely make the permanent count as hands are settled. Similarly, suppose the count is unfavorable, you are dealt soft 17, and the dealer shows a 7. The temporizing count becomes irrelevant and unnecessary: you would never stand with this hand, and you would never double with it against 7.* You save the trouble of taking the temporizing count and merely draw to your soft 17, as prescribed, when it comes time to draw.

In a slightly similar situation, however, the temporizing count may become helpful. Suppose that the dealer shows an Ace instead of a 7 against your soft 17. Once again you will draw (never stand and never double) in this situation, regardless of the count. However, suppose you draw another Ace, making soft 18. Ordinarily you stand with soft 18 against Ace, but in Chapter 8 you will learn that there *is* a time to draw (namely, when the point count is *below* neutral).

If the need to contend with the temporizing count appears an undue additional burden, do not despair. In the

---

*An exception to be presented in Chapter 7 occurs so rarely that it may be ignored for the purpose of this example.

first place, once you are adept at keeping the permanent count, moderate experience will make you reasonably competent at the temporizing count in those situations in which it is helpful. A glance at the various hands at the table often will give you a good estimate of the count. If you sometimes make minor errors—and everyone does—they will not be fatal to your play.

I know from experience that taking the temporizing count is not necessary for proper play of most hands. Usually, something about your hand, the dealer's up-card, the count before the deal, or a combination of these will tell you immediately how you will play the hand. Suppose, for example, you are dealt 11, and the dealer shows a 7. Two other players are at the table, and the count before the deal, fairly early in the deck, is plus 8. You know, of course, that you double down with 11. In Chapter 8, however, we will learn that there are situations when the deck is unfavorable in which we occasionally do not double. But in the example just given, you will know that no possible combination of cards could occur, as the other people draw, that could alter the count so drastically that you would do anything with your 11 except double down. You will not need to dwell on the matter. With only a little experience you will just *know*.

The point count is the backbone of winning play. The temporizing count is a refinement, to make your play more effective, in those situations in which an estimate of the count during the midst of play may affect your decision of what to do.

Count Every Card You Can Count

Much of the following discussion should now be evident from what has preceded. Also, the explanation anticipates later chapters. But even at this point of instruction, best play will be achieved by considering a few additional matters to help in card counting.

Burn Card and Bottom Card

It will be remembered from Chapter 1 that the top card is burned before the deal from a newly shuffled deck is begun. In practice, this custom varies between casinos. Some routinely use a joker face up on the bottom of the deck instead of truly turning a card. Some that follow this practice will also retire the top card to the return tray. In these circumstances there is no opportunity to see and thus to count a burn card. But with the traditional manner of burning the top card, you may get a glimpse of it; if so, it should be counted plus 1 or minus 2, as the case may be.

With most dealers, you will seldom be able to see this burn card. Practice has taught them to move the top card to the bottom, upside down of course, very rapidly, with virtually a sleight-of-hand motion. But some dealers do not bother as much as others to hide the card during this motion, and often they will happen to hold the deck at such an angle that you can see the card being burned if you are watching. I do not recommend watching with too obvious intent; never do anything to advertise unnecessarily that you are counting the cards. But it is not difficult to glance casually toward the dealer's hands at about the time he is ready to burn the card.

At this time occasionally it is also possible to see the bottom card. It is particularly gratifying to have the count on these first two cards before the deal begins, when ordinarily they would simply have to be ignored. Even when a joker is used, and thus no burn card can be counted, you may be able to see the bottom card when the deck is picked up after being cut.

If it seems odd at the moment that the bottom card should be counted just like a played card, even though in a sense it remains in the deck, remember one thing: for practical purposes this card may be regarded as out of the deck. In the first place, practically no casino ever deals the bottom card (I know of only one exception). Even when they deal all the way through the deck before reshuffling, they will not deal the last card. Even if they did so, the bottom card would be "out" of the deck until it was reached. It should be counted if seen.

I have not found that the tendency of some dealers to flash the burn card or bottom card depends particularly on their experience. Some veteran dealers often flash them; some relative beginners virtually never do so. The practice seems to be more a matter of their habit and degree of attention.

Your Neighbors' Cards

Players seated beside you often will hold their hole cards in your full view. These cards should, of course, be incorporated into the temporizing count when this is helpful. There is nothing improper about your looking at your neighbors' hole cards or letting them see yours; you are all playing against the dealer, not against each other. However, I do not recommend craning your neck or engaging in obvious contortions to look at other hands. For one thing, such maneuvers may advertise to the dealer that you are casing the deck. For another, some players may, for personal reasons, resent your looking at their cards.

Cards the Dealer May Hide

Customarily, every card that is played during a hand should eventually be turned up as the bets are settled. In every situation there is a valid reason for the dealer to examine each hand. And the obvious and practical way to do so is simply to turn the cards up on the table in full view of everyone.

Of course, when neither the player nor the dealer has broken, the hands must be exposed for comparison. But even when the dealer breaks, he needs to examine each hand. Obviously, any hand that has drawn cards must be inspected before being paid, to be sure that the hand did not break also. But even a hand that did not draw, and thus must win, must be inspected to be certain it was not a blackjack that an inexperienced player failed to turn up. This is necessary because the payoff for blackjack is greater than for a simple win. For a similar reason, the dealer must inspect each hand when he himself has a blackjack; a black-jack by a player would tie. In addition, the dealer will not accept a player's cards and money if the player simply declares his hand broken and throws the cards in face down. The dealer must inspect them to be sure the player did not misread his hand. The dealer is responsible for seeing that no player cheats himself (or the casino) through ignor-ance of the rules or failure to add a hand correctly.

The one time when there is no obviously valid reason to turn up a face-down card is when every player at the table has broken and the dealer's hand is therefore no longer of any relevance. In this case there is no compelling reason for the dealer to show his hole card, but he customar-ily does so. For one thing, it is a courtesy to the broken players who may simply be curious about what strength hand they were drawing against. Also, it is mechanically convenient to turn up the card in order to add it to other cards the dealer may be holding prior to placing them with the discards.

The custom of turning up all cards in full view is ordinarily followed completely. But some dealers, particularly when they realize that they are confronted by a card-counting player, will adopt certain methods to prevent the player from seeing numerous cards that ordinarily would be exposed to view. The dealer may fail to show his hole card if all players break. When he has a blackjack, he may pick up the players' hands, look at them while keeping their backs to the players, and retire them to the discards. When he breaks, he may check the pat hands for a blackjack in the same manner, never exposing them to view. (Or he may not inspect for players' blackjacks at all. Some casinos claim that Ace,10 is not blackjack unless declared promptly.)

When a dealer adopts these methods of hiding cards, you should counter as much as possible by counting or estimating the hidden cards by inference, as explained previously in this chapter—provided you stay at the table with him at all. If the dealer has an Ace and no blackjack, his other card must be a non-10. A player's pat hand may be *estimated* as minus 1. But be sure the hand was actually being played pat; do not attempt to estimate a simple two-card hand unless the owner gives an indication of its composition. Also, whenever an *unbroken* hand has drawn a 10 or a combination of small cards totaling ten or more, the hole cards must be non-10s.

Of course, if your play is unduly compromised by a dealer who hides cards, it may be expedient to change tables or casinos.

Position

The prior discussion of the temporizing count spoke frequently of adjustments in the count that could be made, based on the cards of players who drew ahead of you. This must have alerted the reader to the advantage of sitting to the left of the other players, since the deal and the drawing of cards proceed clockwise.

Place one, to the dealer's immediate left is known as "first base"; the last place (place six or seven, depending on the size of the table) is spoken of as "third base." (See figure 1, page 3.) I always try to sit near third base, preferably at place five.

The reader may wonder why I do not sit at third base itself. The reason is a practical one: from the vantage point of third base it is difficult to see the cards at the other end of the table. Not only is distance a minor factor, but the dealer's forearms may obscure the cards when he turns them up, particularly the cards at place one (first base). The same thing is true from place six at a seven-place table.

Despite my strong preference for place five, one advantage must be acknowledged for a seat near the right, place two, for example. That is, when the dealer deals down to the last card—and thus must shuffle during the midst of a round—a player near the right will have a better chance of completing his hand (or a major portion of it) from the deck before the shuffle; the dealer will not be able to complete his hand before the shuffle. This tends to be an advantage when the deck is 10-rich. By the same token, it is, of course, a similar disadvantage when the deck is 10-poor. However, bets should be large with a favorable deck and small otherwise. Something can be said, therefore, for sitting near first base instead of near third base.

Nevertheless, I know that the advantage of having a more complete temporizing count at place five more than compensates for the advantage for playing near place one or two. And more to the point, most dealers usually do not deal to the last card; in general, they will shuffle before starting a round if they see they probably do not have enough cards left to complete it. I firmly recommend sitting near third base.

I should mention now that most experts, including myself, prefer an uncrowded table. In fact, most of us prefer to play "head on" against the dealer; that is, to be the only player at the table.

The best thing that can be said for having several players present is that when they play ahead of you, they provide information, via the point count, on how you should play your hand. But several players will obviously bleed away the deck when it is favorable, thus depriving you of a long run of hands from a 10-rich deck. Also, the more players that are present, the more difficult it is to keep an accurate point count. In addition, a crowded table reduces the number of hands you will be able to play during a given period of time. (Since you are a winning player, you should want to play as rapidly and as much as possible.)

A further discussion will be given of this matter in Chapter 10. In some circumstances, there are certain reasons for wanting other players at the table. But these reasons do not nearly compensate for the important advantages of playing at an uncrowded table. The fewer players at the table, the better.

6

Insurance

INTELLIGENT insurance betting is one of the very important—and perhaps the simplest—strategies available to the card-counting Twenty-One player. Insurance was introduced by the casinos as an ingenious scheme to part the player from his money a bit faster, but the skillful player can turn the tables and use the insurance bet, in proper circumstances, as an easy way to increase his profits. Some casinos do not offer it, but it is routinely offered in Las Vegas.

The reader will recall from Chapter 1 the rules of the insurance bet. When the dealer's up-card is an Ace, and thus the threat of a natural (blackjack) exists, the player is given the option of making an insurance bet. The player, of course, will already have made some specific original bet before the cards were dealt. If he now wishes to take insurance, he places an additional bet equal to one-half this original bet. The insurance bet is a wager that the dealer does have a blackjack. If the insurance bet wins, the original bet loses. But since the insurance bet is paid at 2 to 1, the original (lost) bet exactly pays the insurance bet. If the insurance bet loses, the dealer collects it, and play of the hands continues in the usual way. (The different settlement of the insurance bet when both player and dealer have blackjack is discussed later in this chapter.

It will also be remembered (from Chapter 2) that in basic strategy, when the deck is assumed always to be neutral, insurance is a bad bet. It pays only 2 to 1, whereas the true odds are approximately 9 to 4.

But the basis of winning play, as presented in Chapter 3, is that the deck does *not* remain neutral but varies with the ratio of 10s to non-10s. And we have learned that in our point-count system, whenever we reach a count of plus 4, the ratio of 10s to non-10s in the unplayed deck (more precisely, the unseen or uncounted deck) is exactly 1 to 2. Accordingly, whenever insurance is offered, the odds that the dealer's hole card will be a 10, and that he thus will have a blackjack, are precisely 1 to 2 with a plus-4 count. Since the payoff for a winning insurance bet is 2 to 1, it can readily be seen that at plus 4, insurance is an even bet, in the sense that the payoff is at the exact ratio as the correct odds indicate it should be.

The preceding leads to this conclusion: whenever the point count reaches plus 5 or above, insurance is a good bet and should always be taken; the payoff is 2 to 1 on a proposition that will win more than once for each two times it will lose. In other words, the odds of winning are better than one to two. Similarly, insurance should never be taken if the point count is less than plus 4; the payoff is 2 to 1 on a proposition that will win less than once for each two times it will lose.

On the surface, the matter of whether to take insurance when the count is exactly plus 4 seems optional, as the payoff is 2 to 1 on a precisely 1 to 2 proposition. But my advice is ordinarily not to insure at plus 4. Since your capital is limited and the casino's capital is virtually unlimited, chance fluctuations in luck will tend to operate to your disadvantage. Since you will be playing Twenty-One with a definite but moderate advantage and the amount you can afford to lose is limited, a run of bad luck will harm you more than a run of good luck will help you. Propositions that depend entirely on luck should not be accepted gratuitously. And a 1 to 2 chance of winning the insurance bet is purely a break-even proposition—a simple matter of luck.

In playing Twenty-One, of course, you must accept some break-even and even losing propositions (when the point count is neutral or negative), simply to stay in the game. But whether to take insurance is entirely a matter of option, and I recommend doing so only when the point count is above plus 4.

Superstition Versus Fact

Insurance is a side bet, having nothing whatever to do with your original bet or with the hand you have been dealt. It involves only the question of whether the dealer's hole card is or is not a 10. Whether it is a good or bad bet depends on the ratio of 10s to small cards that remain in the unseen deck. That is all there is to it.

Armed with this knowledge, the intelligent player should have no trouble in rejecting the various superstitions he will hear expounded about when to take insurance. The denominator of these superstitions is the unsound belief that the hand the player has been dealt should somehow influence the decision. The commonest is the notion that when the player himself has a blackjack, he should take insurance.

The theory behind this mistake stems from the fact that when a player has blackjack and insures, he will always win something, whereas otherwise he would only tie if the dealer also has blackjack. Players following this strategy seem undisturbed by the fact that they will win only two-thirds as much in the more common situations, when the dealer does not have blackjack.

Many dealers (probably *most* of them) are equally confused about insurance bets. Some of them will gratuitously offer advice to players that a blackjack should be insured. I have no doubt that this counsel is given in perfectly good faith and in an effort to be helpful. Dealers use this peculiar strategy when they themselves play, even though most would not take insurance otherwise.

If we assume an original bet of two chips, the various possibilities follow when the player has a blackjack and the dealer shows an Ace:

A. Player takes insurance, betting one more chip. Dealer has blackjack. Player wins 2 chips on the insurance bet and ties the original bet. Overall, player wins 2 chips.

B. Player takes insurance, betting one more chip. Dealer does not have blackjack. Player loses the insurance bet (1 chip) and wins 1½ times the original bet (3 chips). Overall, player wins 2 chips.

C. Player does not take insurance. Dealer has blackjack. Player ties and breaks even.

D. Player does not take insurance. Dealer does not have blackjack. Player wins 3 chips.

Taking insurance, the player always wins 2 chips. Not taking it, he breaks even 15 times in 49 and wins 3 chips 34 times in 49. In 49 situations of this type, the player who does not insure can expect to win 102 chips (3 x 34 = 102); the player who insures can expect to win only 98 chips (2 x 49 = 98). Obviously, the strategy of always insuring a blackjack is unsound.

In our own system we may or may not insure a blackjack. But the fact that we have a blackjack is irrelevant. We will make the insurance bet if the point count is above plus 4 and not otherwise.

Another common superstition holds: insure good hands but do not insure bad hands. I have even been annoyed by other players at the table offering me this nonsensical advice. Of course, the same fallacy is involved here as with the one about insuring a blackjack. Insurance has nothing to do with the hand that is dealt, *except insofar as that hand influences the temporizing point count.*

Once in downtown Las Vegas, I sat down to play head-on with a dealer, and I was promptly dealt 10,10. The dealer showed an Ace. The point count was minus 3, and I declined insurance. In a few moments the count had changed drastically, to a favorable plus 8 or so, and I was dealt 9,7. Again the dealer had an Ace, and naturally I took insurance. The dealer casually remarked, "I'm surprised you insured a 16 when you didn't insure a 20."

Of course I didn't want him to know I was casing the deck, so I offered a series of "explanations." I said, "I don't always play it the same way." (Hardly! The point count is not always the same.)

This sounded lame, so I added, as play was continuing, "Usually I insure when I have a large bet but not when I have a small one." (Perfectly true. But I did not explain that this is merely because I will usually have a large bet with a high point count and not otherwise.)

Yet I realized that he might soon see that I did not always follow that pattern, as the temporizing count might rapidly change my strategy during the play of a hand. Thus, I continued: "When I had 20, I hoped you didn't have blackjack, so I didn't want to bet you *did* have it. But when I had 16 and took insurance, I *wanted* you to have a blackjack so I could tie. I had a bad hand." (True again. But I did not explain that these wishes were *not* what led me to insure or not.)

The dealer paused to think this over a moment. He said, "Yes, if I were playing, I would certainly want the dealer to have blackjack if I had 16 and could take insurance." He seemed pleased by my explanation. It was obviously the first time he had heard this little reverse twist on the fatuity of insuring good hands but not bad hands.

I should mention this: if other players are at the table, and circumstances somehow make it expedient to explain your "erratic" insurance betting, you will not be very popular if you admit hoping the dealer has a blackjack. However, another ploy is possible. If you have taken insurance with a bad hand and eyebrows are raised, you can merely say, "I was so sure I was going to lose that I just tried to save the money with an insurance bet."

Ordinarily, of course, there is no need to "explain" your strategy. Merely play your own hands as you see fit and let the other players play theirs.

I am certain that much of the confusion surrounding the insurance bet stems from the term *insurance* itself. Since the winning insurance bet exactly restores the losing original bet (except when a player's blackjack is involved), the transaction seems to resemble *insurance* as the term is usually employed. But strictly as a gamble, insuring a car or a house is usually a bad bet. Otherwise, insurance companies could not stay in business. Nevertheless, such insurance may still be a wise investment for a client with limited funds, because he can afford the premium but cannot afford to lose his car or house.

Insurance in this latter circumstance resembles "insurance" in Twenty-One only in the most superficial way. A Twenty-One player who cannot afford to lose the bet on the hand before him is in sad straits indeed. He should never have made the bet in the first place. Also, if he insures a 20 and thus tries to settle, in effect, for half a win to avoid a total loss of the bet, he may end by losing the insurance bet *and* the original bet, provided the dealer draws 21.

If for some odd reason a player were making the one and only bet he ever intended to make, were dealt a blackjack, and the dealer showed an Ace, taking insurance might make a grain of sense. The player would insure a partial win and avoid a tie. But who goes to the casino to play only a single hand?

An Exception

There is *one* circumstance in which your hand should lead you to take insurance. If you have blackjack and the count is exactly plus 4, you should take it. This is the *only* time the old argument for "always winning something" with your blackjack vs. Ace is mathematically sound. The reason is that your capital will always be limited in relation to that of the casino, and insuring a win in this fundamentally break-even situation will tend to stabilize your gambling stake.

I would not bother with this minor matter if it were not for one other advantage of insuring a blackjack: camouflage.* As the dealer will probably become suspicious whenever you fail to insure a blackjack, you certainly should not fail to do so at plus 4. Occasionally, and *purely* for camouflage purposes, you may even want to insure a blackjack at plus 3, even though the maneuver is mathematically unsound. But that is about the limit of this gambit. Always remember what the insurance bet involves: you are not insuring your hand; you are betting on the dealer's hole card.

---

* The principle of camouflage was introduced in Chapter 3 and will be discussed further in Chapter 10.

7

Winning All You Can When You Can

ONE day I fell into conversation with a fellow player, a real high-roller, after we had left the table. We both had won, he by luck and I by design, and we congratulated each other. My acquaintance said, "John, I noticed something about your game. You would win a $20 bet and pull it back. Then, you would lose $5. You kept winning big ones and losing little ones. That's good gambling." Had the cliché not become so weary, I might have replied, "My friend, that's what the game is all about."

Winning large bets while losing small ones *is* the whole point of the game. But you must know *how* to win the large ones.

While previous chapters have described a winning system that will allow you to beat the casinos, the further strategy changes of this chapter will help to provide the really magnificent profits available when the deck is highly favorable. Most of these changes are increasingly aggressive as the point count rises. On the other hand, a few changes are defensive and analogous to standing with hard 15 and 16 against 10 at plus 4, as advised in Chapter 4.

All the changes from basic strategy that were discussed in Chapter 4 will continue to be made at any point count higher than plus 4. Additional ones, however, should be made at plus 8, even more at plus 12, and still more at plus 16. These higher point counts represent 10/X ratios ranging from about 0.6 to about 1.0. The *precise* ratio represented by a particular count higher than plus 4 will vary somewhat with the number of cards that have been dealt, but the counts I have designated for the strategy adjustments provide quite satisfactory approximations. The player's edge with these higher counts ranges from more than 2 percent to about 10 percent and occasionally even more. As the advantage increases, you naturally should tend to increase the size of your bets—within the limits of practicality. The very fact that bets are large gives added importance to the refined strategy I now will present.

Plus 8—An Excellent Deck

When the point count reaches plus 8, indicating a fine 10/X ratio of about 0.6, your percentage advantage is more than double that at plus 4. To exploit the advantage fully, a few further changes in strategy must be made. These are listed in summarized form on pages 87 and 88 but I will first discuss them briefly.

Two adjustments are defensive: stand with hard 16 if the dealer shows 9 (or 10, of course), and in addition to the hard 15 and 16, stand with hard 14 against 10. You are probably going to lose with these hands whatever you do, but you have a slightly better chance if you stand and hope that the dealer has a low hole card than if you risk the probable bust by drawing.

Where surrender is allowed, take advantage of the option in the situations just discussed. You will salvage half your bet, and this is better than either standing or drawing against such a formidable card. Needless to say, you should grit your teeth and draw with 16 against 7, 8, or Ace, and with 14 or 15 against 7, 8, 9, or Ace. In other words, continue basic strategy in all circumstances in which specific strategy adjustments are not recommended.

At plus 8 or above, always double down with 10, regardless of the dealer's up-card. Double down with 8 against 4, in addition to the 5 and 6 as recommended at plus 4.

Double down with soft hands of 13 through 19 against up-cards of 3 through 6. This is a remarkably simple pattern to memorize. The soft-doubling strategy at plus 4 was less symmetrical and required some attention to small details. At plus 8 you simply remember to double with any soft hand of less than 20 against any bust card except 2. (With soft 17 or 18, of course, also continue to double against 2.)

At plus 8 or above split a pair of 10s against 4, 5, or 6. This may seem an astonishing recommendation, but with an excellent, 10-rich deck, the aggressive departure from basic strategy is entirely sound. With a low card, the dealer is even more likely than usual to break. Also, you have an increased possibility of drawing additional 10s for *two* good hands—or even more if the count is high enough to justify resplitting.

A word of caution: the temporizing count becomes vitally important when consideration is given to splitting 10s. Your two 10s themselves will lower the count by four points from the one before the deal; the dealer's 4, 5, or 6 will raise it by only one, for a net of minus three. Thus, in a head-on game or any game in which other players' hands have not been counted, a point count of 11 before the deal will have been needed to justify splitting 10s. If you draw another 10 to your first new hand, as you hope to do, resplitting will not be indicated unless the count before the deal was plus 13 or more.

One other adjustment should be made at plus 8: you will no longer split a pair of 8s if the dealer's up-card is a 10. Merely stand with your unfortunate hard 16 or surrender if possible. Continue to split 8s against all cards except 10.

Plus 12—An Outstanding Deck

When the point count reaches plus 12, the 10/X ratio is about 0.8, and your advantage is about 5 percent. Your bets should be large, and the strategy will be very aggressive —except for a few defensive adjustments if you draw a stiff against a high card.

Stand with hard 16 against Ace (you already know to stand against 9 and 10 in this situation). Stand with hard 15 against 9 or Ace (and against 10, of course). No further changes are made with hard 14; just continue to stand against 10 and play basic strategy against other cards. Stand with hard 13 against 10. With all these stiffs, whenever you would stand against high cards, *surrender if you can.*

Double down with 9 against 8 and with 8 against 2 through 6. These aggressive doubles are merely extensions of previous departures from basic strategy when the dealer has a low card. But also double down with 7 against 5 or 6. Even though you can never make a really good hand by drawing only one card to a 7, the probability that the dealer with a 5 or 6 will break with a point count of plus 12 fully justifies the maneuver.

Double down with all soft hands of 13 through 20, even a soft 20, if the dealer shows 2 through 6. Never mind that your soft 20 is already a good hand. You want to win twice as much with it. You have a fine chance of drawing a 10 for hard 20, but even if you do not, the dealer must draw. He will probably hit a stiff, and the chances are very good that he will break.

The usual variety of suckers at the table may deplore your "foolishness" in doubling with "20" (10), "19" (9), or even soft 18. Never mind: they will be losing and you will be winning. If the dealer is astonished by your play, and often he will be, just be nonchalant: you *want* the dealer to think you are stupid.

At plus 12 or above, split 10s against all bust cards. (We have already learned to split 10s against 4, 5, or 6 at plus 8.) Again the temporizing count must be considered before splitting or resplitting 10s. Each 10 you draw will reduce the point count by two. Nothing more must be learned about splitting 10s. They are *never* split when we think the dealer's hand may already be pat—in other words, never against a 7 or higher card. They are split only against bust cards with a highly favorable, 10-rich deck.

At plus 12 or above, split 9s against all dealer's cards except 10. This strategy is very logical. We split against 2 through 6 and against 8 and 9 for the same reasons given for basic strategy, explained in Chapter 2. But with a highly 10-rich deck, the fine prospect of making two hands of 19 each justifies splitting the 18 (9,9) against 7 (assumed 17) for a double win. And against Ace (he cannot have a 10 in the hole, or he would already have collected), two hands starting with 9 each are better than the original 18 when so many 10s are in the deck. Against 10, of course, we assume a winning 20 by the dealer, stand with the unfortunate 18, and hope for luck; we certainly would never double the bet to try for two 19s when both would be beaten by a pat 20.

A single further adjustment is made at plus 12: split 7s against Ace! This adjustment may seem astonishing, but it represents a sophisticated defensive maneuver. If you have some spare time and want to check on its validity without using complicated mathematics, you may do so by dealing out several hundred experimental hands, as I have done for this and other strategies I recommend.

Give the dealer an Ace and the player two 7s. Remove enough assorted non-10s from the remaining deck to provide a 10/X ratio a bit above 0.8. I recommend a bit above to exaggerate the experimental conditions and to lessen the possibility that statistical variation may give an abnormal result. For demonstration purposes, I suggest removing an Ace, two each of 2s through 6s, a 7, and two each of 8s and 9s. Now deal a few hundred hands in which you draw one card to the 14, stand on the 14, and split the 7s—all this against the Ace and a variety of random non-10 hole cards, making a one chip bet each time. Then compile the results.

You will find that the player will have lost using any strategy, *but he will have lost less by splitting, even though he has had to double his bet each time.*

Thus, it is fortunate that the precise conditions for this strategy maneuver are rare in actual play (you hold 7,7; dealer has Ace; and the 10/X ratio is 0.8 or more). They are *so* rare, in fact, that your overall success will be little affected if you ignore this particular strategy adjustment. Nevertheless, the splitting of 7,7 against Ace with a very high point count provides a further illustration of the so-phistication of this Twenty-One system. Not only does it give strategies to press the advantage of many card holdings. It also recognizes that to be in the game the player must contend with other holdings that will probably lose, and it provides the least unsatisfactory alternatives for managing them.

If you perform the experiment just discussed, you will probably notice another trend: drawing would have lost the player more money than standing. At the moment this fact may seem slightly disturbing. Until now we have learned to draw to hard 14 against Ace. However, for demonstration purposes, we depleted the deck of non-10s almost enough to give a 10/X ratio of 1.0. A bit later we shall see that in this circumstance it is better to stand with hard 14 against Ace than to draw. I should mention also that to perform this experiment for best results, you should play the split hands according to the forthcoming strategy for plus 16.

Plus 16—A Great Deck

When the point count reaches plus 16, your advantage over the casino approaches 10 per cent and sometimes goes even higher. The 10/X ratio is approximately 1.0;* in other words, the deck to be dealt consists of about as many 10s as non-10s.

This desirable circumstance is naturally uncommon. But it occurs often enough that you should be prepared to take full advantage. First, however, learn the defensive adjustments to minimize losses when you hold a stiff against a high card.

Continue the plus-12 strategy as just given and incorpor-

* The astute reader will detect an apparent mathematical error in this figure, but the matter is explained in the discussion of refinements later in this chapter.

ate the following changes: stand with hard 16 against 8 (8,8 is still split against all but 10); stand with hard 14 against 9 or Ace (7,7 against Ace excepted); stand with hard 13 against Ace; and stand with hard 12 against 10 or Ace.

To recapitulate, at plus 16 you will stand: with hard 16 against 8 through Ace (unless the splitting strategy intervenes); with hard 14 or 15 against 9 through Ace (except for splitting 7,7 vs. Ace); and with hard 12 or 13 against 10 or Ace. Surrender in these circumstances if possible. This mass of detail should not be difficult to remember if you have learned the preceding strategies for progressively increasing point counts. If it seems confusing at all, the summary on page 88 will make it easy.

At plus 16, double down with 9 against Ace. You will probably make 19. The dealer will probably either break or make less than 19. Accordingly, go for the double win. Notice that with this magnificently high point count, you double down with 9 against all cards except 9 or 10; *never* double with 9 if the dealer does show 9 or 10.

Double down with 8 against 7. Your expected 18 will beat the dealer's presumed 17.

Double down with 7 against 2 through 4. The reasoning is merely an extension of doubling with 7 against 5 or 6 at plus 12.

Double down with 5 or 6 against 4 through 6! I told you that I would recommend startling strategies. Here, I recommend doubling your bet and restricting yourself to a one-card draw when you cannot possibly make a good hand. But whether your hand is good or bad depends upon what the dealer draws. At plus 16, with 4, 5, or 6, the dealer will probably break. Also, you deprive yourself of very little by restricting your draw to one card; when you draw the expected 10, you would stand even if you *could* draw again. Go ahead and double your bet in an effort to win twice as much.

If you have any doubts about the soundness of this recommendation, conduct an experiment similar to the one I recommended for splitting 7,7 against Ace at high point counts. Take half the non-10s out of a deck. (Be sure these are about equally distributed as to rank.) Then, from the remaining deck, give the dealer a 5 and the player a 3,2 or 4,2 (3s should be split as usual). Deal a few hundred hands, giving the player one card each time and the dealer a random unknown hole card dealt each time from the depleted deck. Play out each hand: the dealer must draw to 16 or less. Under these circumstances, the player must surely win in the long run. But of greater importance, he will win *more* than if he fails to double the bet, thus retaining the option to draw extra cards.

I should mention that when you double down with hard 5 or 6, you will be regarded as an idiot. Most dealers will caution you against such "foolishness." But I say again, you *want* the dealer to think you are crazy. Just say, "I've decided to bet you will break. Give me a card down." It is when the dealer does *not* question your decision that you should be concerned. That dealer probably recognizes expert play.

At plus 16 or above, double down with soft 17 against 7. This is the *one* circumstance in which a soft hand warrants doubling when the dealer is not showing a bust card. At this high point count, he probably has 17, and you will probably make hard 17 for a tie. But you *may* be lucky and draw a low card for a double win. Other possibilities tend to cancel each other. The conditions for this maneuver occur so rarely that you may ignore it if it burdens your memory.

At plus 16 or above, do not split 2s or 3s against 7. (Continue to split against 2 through 6.)

Summary

With high point counts, continue all the changes from basic strategy recommended for the plus-4 strategy (Chapter 4) and also do the following.

At plus 8 or above:
    Stand with hard 16 vs. 9 (or 10).*
    Stand with hard 14 (or hard 15 or 16, of course) vs. 10.*
    Always double down with 10.
    Double down with 8 vs. 4, 5, or 6.
    Double down with soft 13 through soft 19 vs. 3 through 6. (Do not forget soft 17 and soft 18 vs. 2.)
    Split 10s vs. 4 through 6 (*Remember the temporizing count.*)
    Do not split 8s vs. 10.*
At plus 12 or above, follow the preceding rules and also:
    Stand with hard 16 vs. 9 through Ace.*
    Stand with hard 15 vs. 9 through Ace.*
    Hard 14 strategy is unchanged, except for 7,7.
    Stand with hard 13 vs. 10.*
    Double down with 9 vs. 2 through 8.
    Double down with 8 vs. 2 through 6.
    Double down with 7 vs. 5 or 6.
    Double down with soft 13 through soft 20 vs. 2 through 6.
    Split 10s vs. 2 through 6. (Again, remember the temporizing count.)
    Split 9s vs. everything but 10.
    Split 7s vs. Ace.

---

*Surrender if possible.

At plus 16 or above follow the preceding rules and also:
    Stand with hard 16 vs. 8 through Ace.*
    Hard 15 strategy is unchanged.
    Stand with hard 14 vs. 9 through Ace* (except 7,7 vs. Ace—see preceding).
    Stand with hard 13 vs. 10 or Ace.*
    Stand with hard 12 vs. 10 or Ace.*
    Double down with 9 vs. everything except 9 and 10.
    Double down with 8 vs. 2 through 7.
    Double down with 7 vs. 2 through 6
    Double down with 5 or 6 (3,3 excepted) vs. 4 through 6.
    Double down with soft 17 vs. 7.
    Do not split 2s or 3s vs. 7.

These strategy changes are recapitulated in table I (page 103).

Refinements

At this stage of instruction, review and practice until you can employ the strategy adjustments for a favorable deck without hesitation or uncertainty. Once you can do so, a few refinements will add a bit of precision to your game and permit extra profits. After considering these, we will move on to a presentation of adjustments to help preserve your money when the 10/X ratio is *un*favorable.

The Varying Significance of the Point Count

As mentioned before, a plus-4 point count *always* indicates a 0.5 ratio of 10s to non-10s among the uncounted cards.

On the other hand, all other point counts represent a somewhat different ratio when most cards have been counted

---
*Surrender if possible.

from that when only a few have been counted. You may
wonder, then, why I should recommend a particular playing strategy at, say, plus 8 or plus 12, when these counts
do not have a consistent significance. The reason is that
they give sufficiently accurate approximations of the 10/X
ratio to avoid leading you into serious errors. True, if the
first eight cards dealt were all non-10s, the point count of
plus 8 would not *quite* correspond to a 10/X ratio of 0.6;
plus 9 would really be needed at this stage through the
deck. However, *most* of the strategy changes recommended
at plus 8 would still be fully justified, and the few others
would be *nearly* correct. Also, in the more common circumstance when plus 8 occurs after just a few more cards have
been dealt and about three-fourths of the deck remains,
plus 8 will represent just about precisely 0.6.

If plus 8 occurs with half the deck counted and half
remaining, the count will really represent a slightly *more*
favorable 10/X ratio than normal; a point count of plus 7
would be adequate to justify the strategy changes ordinarily
reserved for plus 8. Similarly, if three-fourths of the deck
has been counted and the dealer is still dealing the remaining
cards, *plus 6* will be adequate to justify the plus-8 strategy!*

Notice that you are never *badly* in error by playing the
plus-8 strategy only at plus 8 and above. Plus 12 involves
an analogous series of considerations. It will not quite represent an 0.8 ratio if it occurs at the earliest possible moment,
but it almost will. In the commoner situations when plus
12 occurs, with the deck about half depleted, it will represent just about exactly 0.8. Only when a very few cards

---

* For an estimate of the degree of deck depletion, glance at the discards
in the return tray; if no tray is used, you can estimate the degree of
depletion by glancing at the side of the deck in the dealer's palm. The
discarded portion will usually have a slightly different hue from the
undealt portion, and a break can be seen between the two.

remain to be dealt will it represent a ratio significantly more favorable.

With high point counts, there is seldom any real need to pay attention to the size of the remaining deck for the purpose of appraising the varying significance of the point count. If you wish, you may improve your results slightly by shading your point-count requirement downward by a point in playing the plus-8 strategy with the deck half or more depleted. Do the same with the plus-12 strategy if the deck is *substantially more* than half depleted (shade down even by a couple of points if *very* few cards, say less than a dozen, remain uncounted). But only with the plus-16 strategy does the significance of the count vary much when few cards remain. This count rarely occurs until more than half the deck is dealt. (If it occurs much earlier, shade your requirements upward by a couple of points before invoking the strategy changes.) And when *very* few cards remain uncounted (say about half a dozen are face down on the table, and the dealer has about the same number left in his hand), you may shade the requirements for the plus-16 strategy downward by four or five points. Invoke it at about plus-12. In other words, if you have counted at least three-fourths of the deck, approximately half of the remaining cards will be 10s even with a count a few points below plus 16.

Plus 16 is a grosser approximation than the other point counts designated until now. It nevertheless is quite satisfactory: it *cannot* occur very early in the deck; it seldom does so until more than half the cards are dealt; and most dealers will shuffle when the deck is sufficiently depleted to allow you otherwise to use the refined end play just discussed.

This consideration of the varying significance of the point count largely anticipates matters in Chapter 8. There we will deal with negative point counts and an unfavorable deck. We shall see that severe swings occur in the significance of designated counts when the deck nears depletion. But that can wait until the next chapter. With favorable decks, merely note that if a high point count occurs at the earliest possible moment, it is not quite as favorable as when it occurs with a considerably depleted deck. Refinements in appraising its significance are rarely of any real importance unless it is in the two-figure range with no more than one-fourth of the deck remaining to be dealt.

A glance ahead to figure 4 (page 106) should give some insight into the varying significance of the point count.

Plus-3 Strategy

In considering the transitions in strategy made at plus 4, plus 8, plus 12, and plus 16, you probably wondered whether any of the changes could properly have been made with some point count intermediate between neutral and plus 4, between plus 4 and plus 8, et cetera. The answer is yes—a few. But remember that this Twenty-One method often involves approximations; pinpoint precision is unnecessary and would be extremely difficult to learn. If you like, however, you can sometimes employ a substrategy of some importance by making a few changes at plus 3 that are normally reserved for plus 4.

Suppose the deck is freshly shuffled, and you are dealt 7,5. The dealer turns up a 3. In basic strategy you would draw; at plus 4 you would stand. But notice that the very cards in this example that give you your 12, together with the dealer's 3, combine to give a temporizing count of plus 3. Ordinarily a count of plus 3 is really enough to make it advisable to stand with hard 12 against 3 (although not against 2).

A few other combinations of small cards warrant adopting the plus-4 strategy at plus 3, provided the undealt deck is not greatly depleted. You would not want to stand on hard 12 against 3, however, if enough hands had been dealt to deplete the deck beyond half way. We have just discussed the varying significance of the point count depending on the size of the undealt (uncounted) deck. Remember a similar matter from Chapter 3: when the deck is one-fourth depleted, plus 1, instead of zero, indicates a *precisely* neutral deck; when it is half dealt, plus 2 indicates the same; and when it is three-fourths dealt, plus 3 does so.

But the reason the special plus-3 strategy is fairly important is that you often will count only three small cards before making your strategy decision on the first hand after the deck is shuffled. In addition to standing with 12 against 3, double down with hard 8 against 5 or 6, and double down with soft 17 against 2.

At a crowded table, use the preceding strategy only on the first hand after the shuffle. With just a couple of other players present, use it with a temporizing count of plus 3 on the second hand. And in a head-on game, use it for the first four or five hands.

Two other strategy changes appropriate at plus 3 differ from the ones just discussed. They do not involve just three small cards, but hands in which the dealer turns up a 10. Nevertheless, they are so firmly indicated at any 10/X ratio above neutral that they can almost always be used with a temporizing count of plus 3, regardless of how far the deck is depleted.

One occurs fairly commonly: stand with hard 16 against 10. This variation from basic strategy is really indicated with any 10/X ratio above neutral. Thus, it should be invoked at plus 3 in any circumstance unless the deck is almost fully depleted.

(For extra precision, stand at plus 2 if the deck is no more than half depleted. In fact, on the first hand after the shuffle, if the temporizing count is otherwise zero, you are justified in standing against 10 whenever the first card you draw brings your total to hard 16; in other words, stand at plus 1.)

A less important but interesting point: stand with 7,7 against 10 if the point count is plus 3, *regardless* of how far the deck is depleted. (In casinos that allow surrender, always do so if the strategy otherwise calls for standing with a stiff against a high card. Surrender with 7,7 against 10 in the circumstance just discussed.) In other words, this variation is actually justified with a neutral deck. I could have included this variation as a component of the basic strategy, but I wanted to avoid such rarely occurring sophistications that might complicate the presentation at that stage of instruction.

A summary of the special plus-3 strategy follows:

Stand with hard 16 vs. 10* (unless the deck is greatly depleted).**
Stand with 7,7 vs. 10.**
Stand with hard 12 vs. 3*** (if the deck is only slightly depleted).
Double down with 8 vs. 5 or 6 (if the deck is only slightly depleted).
Double down with soft 17 vs. 2 (if the deck is only slightly depleted).

The preceding are refinements, of course. They are not vital to winning play. If they seem too complicated at the moment, defer them for later review.

---

*8,8 excepted.
**Surrender if possible.
***6,6 excepted.

Surrender When in Doubt

Except in basic strategy, I have recommended that the surrender option merely preempt the strategy for standing with stiffs against high cards. That satisfactory approximation to best strategy eliminates undue preoccupation with an option that usually is unavailable. As a refinement, however, I suggest that you surrender one point or so below the one previously recommended.

Instead of burdening your memory now with a whole new surrender strategy, you may choose to do what I do: in borderline situations, when I have a doubtful decision, I surrender and save half the bet. Be careful, however, not to exaggerate the problem. That is what leads bad players to surrender far too often. Just surrender if the decision is truly doubtful.

Splitting 4s in Northern Nevada

In most casinos of northern Nevada, doubling down is severely restricted. Doubling often is not allowed with hands of less than 10. On rare occasions, this rule leads an expert player to reconsider the manner of playing a pair of 4s.

At plus 12, we have learned to double down with 8 against small cards. But if house rules forbid this, and the 8 consists of 4,4, consideration may be given to splitting. At precisely plus 12, I recommend splitting the 4s only against 5 or 6. However, at plus 16, split 4s against 2 through 6.

Doubling Down with Soft Hands in Northern Nevada

In casinos in which doubling down is forbidden with less than 10, it obviously is forbidden with soft hands in general. The rule thus deprives you of the basic strategy.

Remember, however, that with a plus-12 deck or better, we double with soft 20 against 2 through 6. And soft 20 may be considered a 10. Thus, you *can* double down in certain favorable situations that might be overlooked. (If a casino allows doubling with 9 but forbids it with lower totals, further opportunities are available with soft 19.)

Because of a practical matter, this discussion is little more than academic. In casinos where doubling with soft hands is generally not seen, you will call much attention to yourself if you insist on doubling with a soft 20. The dealer (and pit bosses) *may* think you are merely addled, but more likely they will suspect that you are an expert player—an undesirable consequence. It may be wise, for camouflage purposes, to forego the better play and stand.*

The Sad Estate of a Pair of Sevens

Why is 7,7 so often handled differently from another hard 14? The reason is that with 8,6, 9,5, 10,4, et cetera, four uncounted 7s may remain in the undealt deck, any one of which would add to make 21 after a draw. But if the 14 is made of 7,7, two of the 7s are being used already.

The object of the game is to beat the dealer, and the best way to do so is to make 21. When half the 7s are gone, the possibilities of winning by drawing to 14 are much reduced.

Accordingly, we stand with 7,7 at times when we would otherwise draw to 14. Under the same circumstances, we surrender if possible. The paucity of 7s in the deck greatly influences the decision to split 7,7 against Ace at a point count of plus 12 and is a factor in the other strategies for splitting 7s.

---

*Since a two-card soft 21 is blackjack, and since a rule allowing doubling with more than two cards has virtually disappeared, little attention needs to be given to doubling with soft 21. However, if a casino does allow doubling after cards have been drawn, soft 21 would warrant doing so against 2 through 6 if the 10/X ratio were more favorable than 1.0 — in other words, if the point count were just slightly above plus 16.

8

Guarding Your Money When You Must

I heard a fellow say, "I went to Las Vegas and broke even. And boy, I sure can use the money!"

Our goal is somewhat more ambitious than his. But if we were forced to play all our hands under the conditions considered in this chapter, we could appreciate his sentiment.

Roughly speaking, the deck is unfavorable in terms of the 10/X ratio (an abnormally high number of small cards will remain in the undealt deck) about one-third of the time during typical play. Thus, merely to be in the game, you must be prepared to play about this fraction of your hands at a slight disadvantage. Fortunately, adjustments in strategy are available to allow you to keep this disadvantage very low and preserve your capital for aggressive betting during that third of the time when the 10/X ratio varies in the other direction to your advantage. (Under average conditions, you will find the deck neutral in playing the other third of your hands, and you will use basic strategy.)

For practical purposes, you may assume that your disadvantage will never be much worse than 2 percent. Note how this figure contrasts with the high percentage advantages you frequently achieve with a favorable deck. But with *any* disadvantage, your bets naturally should be small. On the next several pages we also shall see that we should draw to stiffs more often than usual (fewer bust cards will remain in the deck); we should double down less often; and overall, we should split fewer pairs. Insurance, of course, should never be taken. Surrender should be avoided (with two borderline exceptions, to be discussed on pages 105 and 107).

Negative Point Counts—A Poor Deck

When the point count is below zero, you should make certain variations from basic strategy to minimize your disadvantage. With these adjustments, your disadvantage will be almost trivial provided the point count drops only slightly below neutral—less than 1 percent at the 10/X ratio of about 0.4 now under consideration.

Always draw to hard 12, regardless of the dealer's card (6,6 is excepted, of course, when the strategy calls for splitting). Draw to hard 13 if the dealer shows a 2 or 3. Notice that the pattern is reminiscent of basic strategy; a similar pattern will appear in a subsequent series of strategy adjustments.

Draw to soft 18 against Ace. You will remember from Chapter 2, in which I advised drawing to soft 18 against 9 or 10, that I said whether also to draw against Ace was a borderline decision in basic strategy. With a point count below neutral to any degree, we do so.

With a 10-poor deck, do not double down with 11 against Ace; do not double with 10 against 9 or Ace; and do not double with 9 against 2 or 3. The relative lack of 10s in the remaining deck reduces the chance of making a good hand with one draw; the excessive number of small cards will reduce the danger of breaking if the first draw should make a total that would indicate another.

Doubling down with soft hands should be restricted: double with soft 17 and soft 18 only against 4, 5, or 6; double with soft 14, 15, or 16 only against 5 or 6; and no longer double with soft 13 at all. Remember that doubling with soft hands is based in large part on the hope that the dealer will break. He is less likely to do so when excessive small cards are in the deck. Also, these small cards increase the possibility that you may find it expedient to draw more than one card; this factor partially determines the precise pattern of the strategy adjustments recommended.

A few changes in pair-splitting strategy are advisable even with a slightly unfavorable 10/X ratio: do not split Aces against Ace; do not split 9s, 6s, 3s, or 2s against 2; but do split 3s against 8. If you forget these recommendations for splitting, no great harm will result; the precise circumstances occur rarely.

A summary of the strategy changes with a poor deck is given on pages 101 and 102.

Minus 8—A Bad Deck

A minus-8 point count indicates a 10/X ratio of approximately 0.3. Without strategy adjustments, the player's disadvantage would be very substantial with this bad deck. With appropriate strategy, however, it can probably be held below 2 percent.

In addition to the changes discussed for any negative count, always draw to hard 13 or hard 14. Also draw to hard 15 against 2 or 3. Notice again the reemerging pattern. And also consider the drastic change from basic strategy in handling stiffs: we now stand only on hard 15 against 4, 5, or 6 and hard 16 against 2 through 6; all other stiffs are hit (unless the pair-splitting strategy intervenes).

Draw to hard 17 against Ace. With this 10-poor deck, a dealer holding the versatile Ace is *very* unlikely to break. But the large number of small cards give you a fighting chance of drawing a 2, 3, or 4 for a good hand. This strategy change is not too important, as the need for it occurs so rarely, and your bets will be small when it does. But once again, it illustrates something I told you before: expert play often involves measures that astonish the ignorant. If you are scolded for your "foolishnesss" in drawing to 17, just say sheepishly, "I misread my hand."

Double down with 10 or 11 only against 2 through 7. No longer double with 9 against anything.

Soft hands seldom warrant doubling down with a minus-8 point count, but continue to double with soft 18 against 5, with soft 17 against 5 or 6, and with soft 16 against 6.

Pair splitting, with its increased investment, is further restricted with a minus-8 point count. Split Aces only against 2 through 7; split 9s only against 5 or 9; split 6s only against 5 or 6; and no longer split 2s against 3.

A summary of the strategy changes with a bad deck is given on page 101.

Minus 16—A Very Bad Deck

With a minus-16 point count, the player is at a disadvantage of at least 2 percent, but by using my method, he should not be much worse off than that figure. Without the strategy adjustments of this chapter, however, prospects would be hopeless. Minus 16 indicates a 10/X ratio of about 0.2 or worse: very few 10s remain in the undealt deck, and small cards abound.

At minus 16, hit *all* stiffs. In playing hard hands, use the strategy of those fools who mimic the dealer (unless you have a pair that should be split). In other words, draw to hard 12 through hard 16, regardless of the dealer's card.

With a very bad, minus-16 deck, do not double down with any hand—hard or soft. You will probably lose twice your money with a single draw; you may very well make a good hand if you reserve the right to draw as many cards as you wish.

In general, pair splitting is further restricted: do not split Aces at all, regardless of the dealer's card; merely draw to the soft 12 (2). Also, do not split 9s or 6s against anything and do not split 8s against an Ace.

A pair of 3s receives rather peculiar handling with unfavorable decks. You will remember from Chapter 2 that this pair is basically split against 2 through 7. At any negative point count, I recommended splitting against 8 but no longer against 2. Now, with the very bad deck of minus 16, we should also split 3s against 9 or 10—in other words, against every card but 2 and Ace.

We now have considered a series of strategy changes in which we progressively altered the pair-splitting strategy as the deck became less favorable. You can see that the only pairs that are still split with a very bad deck are 2s, 3s, 7s, and 8s. All of these except the 7s are split in a pattern differing from that dictated by basic strategy.

Pair-splitting strategy admittedly is more difficult to learn than others: it lacks the neat patterns seen with most; also, the specific situations for changes occur less often and thus provide less practice in actual play. However, this latter feature makes the strategy changes somewhat less vital to successful play than the others, particularly with an unfavorable deck. If they overtax your memory at the moment, refer to the simplified rules of thumb given on pages 108 and 109. Eventually, however, you will need to learn the strategy fairly well as presented heretofore; it will save you a bit of money from time to time.

Summary

With negative point counts, modify the basic strategy as follows.

At any negative count:
    Always draw to hard 12 (except when 6,6 is split).
    Draw to hard 13 vs. 2 or 3 (i.e., vs. every card but 4,5, or 6).
    Draw to soft 18 vs. 9, 10, and Ace.
    Do not double with 11 vs. Ace (but continue vs. all other cards).
    Do not double with 10 vs. 9 (only vs. 2 through 8).
    Do not double with 9 vs. 2 or 3 (only vs. 4, 5, and 6).
    Do not double with soft 17 or 18 vs. 3 (only vs. 4, 5, and 6).
    Do not double with soft 14, 15, or 16 vs. 4 (only vs. 5 and 6).
    Do not double with soft 13 at all.
    Do not split Aces against Ace (but continue against all other cards).
    Do not split 9s, 6s, 3s, or 2s vs. 2.
    Split 3s vs. 8 (i.e., vs. 3 through 8).
    Ordinarily, do not surrender (see pages 105 and 107 for exceptions).

At minus 8 or below, follow the preceding rules and also:
    Always draw to hard 13 and 14 (except when 7,7 is split).
    Draw to hard 15 vs. 2 or 3 (i.e., vs. every card but 4,5, or 6.)
    Draw to hard 17 vs. Ace.

Double with 10 or 11 vs. only 2 through 7.
Do not double with 9 at all.
Double with soft 18 only vs. 5.
Double with soft 17 only vs. 5 or 6.
Double with soft 16 only vs. 6.
Do not double with any other soft hands.
Split Aces only vs. 2 through 7.
Split 9s only vs. 5 or 9.
Split 6s only vs. 5 or 6.
Do not split 2s vs. 3.
Never surrender.

At minus 16 or below, follow the preceding rules and also:
Always draw to hard 15 and 16 (i.e., hit *all* stiffs—hard 12 through 16).
Do not double down with any hand, hard or soft.
Do not split Aces, 9s, or 6s vs. anything.
Do not split 8s vs. Ace (continue to split vs. 2 through 10).
Split 3s vs. 9 and 10 (now vs. 3 through 10).

These strategy changes are recapitulated in table 1 (page 103).

Refinements

There are several variations of play with a 10-poor deck that can increase efficiency.

The Varying Significance of the Point Count

In the following discussion of negative point counts, please bear in mind that in speaking of counts *below* the one specified, we mean a larger negative number. Recall that in the earlier portion of this chapter, changes from basic strategy were recommended with any negative point count (minus 1

Point Count*

	−16	−8	<0	0	+4	+8	+12	+16
Hard Hands — Draw								
>17								
17	A	A						
16	2-A	7-A	7-A	7-A	7-9/A	7-8/A	7-8	7
15	2-A	2-3/7-A	7-A	7-A	7-9/A	7-9/A	7-8	7-8
14	2-A	2-A	7-A	7-A	7-A	7-9/A	7-9/A	7-8
13	2-A	2-A	2-3/7-A	7-A	7-A	7-A	7-9/A	7-9
12	2-A	2-A	2-A	2-3/7-A	7-A	7-A	7-A	7-9
<12	2-A	2-A	2-A	2-A	2-A	2-A	2-A	2-A
Hard Hands — Double**								
11		2-7	2-10	2-A	2-A	2-A	2-A	2-A
10		2-7	2-8	2-9	2-9	2-A	2-A	2-A
9			4-6	2-6	2-7	2-7	2-8	2-8/A
8					5-6	4-6	2-6	2-7
7							5-6	2-6
5 or 6								4-6
Soft Hands — Draw								
>18								
18	9-A	9-A	9-A	9-10	9-10	9-10	9-10	9-10
<18	2-A	2-A	2-A	2-A	2-A	2-A	2-A	2-A
Soft Hands — Double**								
20							2-6	2-6
19					5-6	3-6	2-6	2-6
18		5	4-6	3-6	2-6	2-6	2-6	2-6
17		5-6	4-6	3-6	2-6	2-6	2-6	2-7
16		6	5-6	4-6	4-6	3-6	2-6	2-6
15			5-6	4-6	4-6	3-6	2-6	2-6
14			5-6	4-6	4-6	3-6	2-6	2-6
13				4-6	4-6	3-6	2-6	2-6
Pairs — Split***								
A,A		2-7	2-10	2-A	2-A	2-A	2-A	2-A
10,10						4-6	2-6	2-6
9,9		5/9	3-6/8-9	2-6/8-9	2-6/8-9	2-6/8-9	2-9/A	2-9/A
8,8	2-10	2-A	2-A	2-A	2-A	2-9/A	2-9/A	2-9/A
7,7	2-7	2-7	2-7	2-7	2-7	2-7	2-7/A	2-7/A
6,6		5-6	3-7	2-7	2-7	2-7	2-7	2-7
5,5								
4,4								
3,3	3-10	3-8	3-8	2-7	2-7	2-7	2-7	2-6
2,2	4-7	4-7	3-7	2-7	2-7	2-7	2-7	2-6

Interior figures represent dealer's up-card.

Take insurance > +4. For surrender strategy, see text.

*Except for +4, point counts are approximate; see text & figure 4, page 106.

**When rules forbid doubling down, follow strategy for drawing.

***When apparent contradictions occur, follow strategy for pair splitting.

Table 1. Master Strategy Table

or below), but still others were added for counts reaching minus 8 or below, and still others for minus 16 or below.

These transition points are reasonably satisfactory with a relatively undepleted deck, since their relationship to a specified 10/X ratio varies only moderately. They are just about precisely correct in a common circumstance when they are useful: the second round at a moderately crowded table—in other words, when about one-third of the cards have been counted or estimated into the temporizing count. On the first round after shuffling at a less crowded table (first three or so in a head-on game), you will increase your accuracy somewhat if you will wait for a count one unit below those previously recommended before invoking the changes specified. The only matter of real importance, as it occurs often, involves the initial changes from basic strategy indicated with any negative point count: if no more than about one-fourth of the deck has been counted, insist on minus 2 instead of minus 1.

As the deck continues to be depleted, enormous changes occur in the significance of negative point counts. "Enormous" may be a misnomer when the previously considered minus-1 changes are involved, but if half the deck has been dealt, these changes should be invoked with a zero point count. They should be put into effect at plus 1 if the deck is much more than half depleted!

The changes recommended at minus 8 should be made with any negative count if the deck is much more than half dealt (only at minus 3 or so if it is near exactly half depleted). If the deck is half depleted, the changes previously recommended at minus 16 should be made at minus 8.

Finally, suppose the dealer is almost out of cards and only few uncounted ones are face down on the table. In this circumstance, plus 2 is low enough for the initial changes. Far more important, the changes earlier reserved for minus 8 are fully indicated at zero. And the extreme changes ordinarily made at minus 16 should be made at about minus 3 or below.

Thus, with an unfavorable deck, the point count varies greatly in significance when the deck is depleted, in contrast to the relatively moderate variation with a favorable deck. The reason is that, in this system, each 10 contributes twice as much in the negative direction as each non-10 in the positive, and there are far fewer 10s than non-10s. If these instructions appear complicated at first, just notice that as the deck becomes depleted, the ranges between strategy changes cluster more and more narrowly near plus 4. However, this clustering does not become severe until the deck is more than half dealt.

Figure 4 provides a convenient visual aid to give guidance to the varying significance of the point count.

The money you will save in unfavorable situations will reward you many times over if you will pay careful attention to learning this refinement. With extremely unfavorable decks, you will hold many stiffs against small cards; you will hold many hands that ordinarily would lead you to double down; and you will occasionally hold a pair that deserves reconsideration before splitting, drawing, or standing. In these situations, your knowledge that the undealt deck is loaded with small cards can equip you with a properly stingy method of end play.

Rarely Surrender with a Negative Point Count

In Chapter 2 (basic strategy) I advised you to surrender with hard 15 or 16 against 10 (provided, of course, you happen to be in one of the relatively few casinos in which surrender is allowed). Earlier in this chapter I generally advised against any surrender with a negative point count. However, the very cards that compose many 15s and 16s—10,5 and 10,6—to-

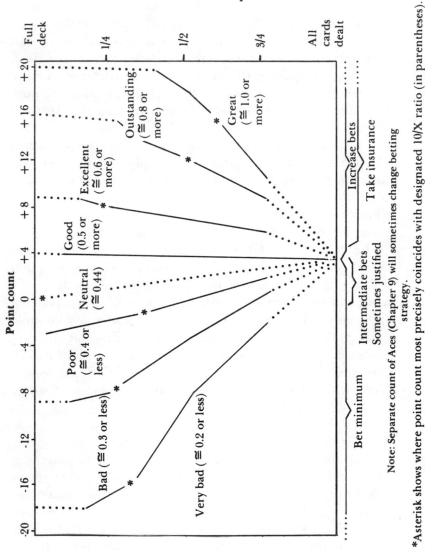

Figure 4. The Changing Significance of the Point Count

gether with the dealer's 10 will give a minus-3 temporizing count on the first hand after the shuffle. These circumstances comprise the exceptions that I promised earlier to discuss: with a nearly full deck, go ahead and surrender.

Naturally, in view of the discussion just completed of the varying significance of the point count, you would not want to surrender at minus 3 after the deck becomes depleted. However, you can still surrender at a point or two below *neutral*—provided you bear in mind that the count indicating neutrality (10/X of 0.44) gradually rises slightly in the positive direction as the deck becomes progressively more depleted.

Two Intermediate Strategies

Please recall the pattern of adjustments for drawing to stiffs with progressively unfavorable point counts: draw to 12 against anything and to 13 against 2 or 3 with any negative count; draw also to 13 and 14 against anything and to 15 against 2 or 3 at minus 8; and draw to all stiffs against anything at minus 16. If you suspected that some similar, intermediate adjustments might properly be made somewhere near the middle of these rather wide ranges of point count, you were correct.

I limited the presentation to only three groups of adjustments in the negative range as a matter of convenience and to avoid burdening you with undue tedium. The only sacrifice in precision of any real importance involved the matter of drawing to stiffs against low cards. You can improve your effectiveness somewhat if you will draw to hard 13 against anything and to hard 14 against 2 or 3 when the point count drops a bit beyond halfway in the excursion between zero and minus 8. In other words, use this strategy at about minus 5 (wait for minus 6 very early in the deck, and shade the requirement toward zero when the deck is nearly depleted).

Similarly, at minus 12, draw to hard 15 against anything and to hard 16 against 2 or 3. Again, shade the requirement by several points toward zero near the end of the deck.

If you ignore these two refinements, no great harm will result. However, once you have mastered the principal material of this chapter, adopting the refinements should follow easily, as they repeat a pattern previously introduced.

A Rough Approximation of Pair-Splitting Strategy

The pair-splitting strategy of basic (neutral) strategy is very important to winning play, and the need to vary this strategy with changes in point count is relatively uncommon. However, many different *rare* combinations of cards and point count that indicate a change in strategy do occur, and most occur with negative counts.

Since the splitting strategy with favorable point counts (Chapter 7) involves large bets, it is wise to learn it rather carefully. You would not want to squander money on unsound splits or to sacrifice winnings or defensive adjustments when they are available. Also, there really are not very many changes to learn with positive point counts anyway.

If, however, in your earlier sessions of using the Archer Method, pair splitting with unfavorable point counts causes a problem, it is reasonably satisfactory to restrict this phase of the game to a few rules of thumb that either cover or reasonably approximate the more frequent requirements.

Simply remember the following:

1. Split Aces only against 2 through 7 when the point count indicates a bad, minus-8* deck or worse.
2. Discontinue all splitting of 9s and 6s when the point count indicates a bad, minus-8* deck or worse.

---

*Remember that the specific point-count designations are precise only in certain circumstances; see figure 4.

3. Otherwise, play the basic strategy for pair splitting.

Obviously, these rules of thumb only roughly approximate best strategy. But the more frequently occuring errors they introduce are relatively unimportant, and the serious ones occur rarely. It is, of course, desirable to master the complete pair-splitting strategy.

The Reverse Point Count

While most dealers do not deal to the last card before shuffling, some continue to do so—occasionally or frequently. They are more likely to deal to the last card when the table is crowded, and that is the time the subject of the following discussion is most useful.

Remember that when the deck is exhausted during the midst of a round, and thus the cards are shuffled to complete the round, the point count reverts to zero. The cards remaining on the table will be counted at the showdown and will provide the new count.

In this circumstance, however, it usually is possible to infer the exact or approximate point count represented by all the cards remaining on the table at the time of the shuffle—even though the hole cards are hidden. This count should be taken whenever the temporizing count is relevant to proper play of the hand.

I call the count in this particular situation the *reverse point count*. It is derived as follows. When all discards have been counted and are being shuffled to complete a round, the point count they represent, combined with the count of all cards remaining in play, must equal plus 4. Accordingly, any difference between the count and plus 4 at the time of the shuffle will convert to a temporizing count of this quantity in the opposite positive or negative direction from plus 4. For example:

With plus 7:   7 - 4 =   3.The count reverses to minus 3.
With minus 3:   -3 - 4 = -7.The count reverses to plus 7.
With plus 3:   3 - 4 = -1.The count reverses to plus 1.
With plus 1:   1 - 4 = -3.The count reverses to plus 3.
With plus 4:   4 - 4 =   0.The count reverses to zero.
With zero: 0 - 4 = -4.The count reverses to plus 4.
With plus 12:   12 - 4 = 8   The count reverses to minus 8.

With minus 12: -12 - 4 = -16. The count reverses to plus 16.

Consider this brain teaser: Does plus 2 reverse? Mathematically, yes, because 2 - 4 = -2. As in the preceding examples, change the negative quantity to positive. Thus plus 2 "reverses" to plus 2. Actually, the matter is not entirely academic. Because of the varying significance of the point count, plus 2 with a greatly depleted deck represents a slightly unfavorable 10/X ratio. But after the shuffle, with the deck restored to nearly full, the significance of plus 2 reverses to represent a slightly favorable ratio.

To illustrate the practical value of the reverse point count, suppose the count before the deal from a partial deck is a favorable plus 10. A round of hands is dealt to several players and the dealer, but the deck is exhausted before the draws can be completed, and no busts or blackjacks have occurred. The dealer pulls out the last card—say a 10—and retracts it. If you are alert, you will simultaneously glimpse the burn card remaining face up in his palm—say a 4.* The count of all the cards going into the shuffle will thus be plus 9. Accordingly, all the cards remaining in play must represent a point count of minus 5 (9 - 4 = 5, which reverses to -5). For the purpose of playing your hand, then, the deck should be regarded as unfavorable, not favorable, as the count before

---

*Whenever you have been able to count the bottom card or burn card early in the game, try to remember not to count it again.

the deal would have indicated. For example, suppose you hold 5,3, and the dealer shows 6. With a 10-rich deck, you would double. But the reverse point count has shown the undealt deck, after the shuffle, to have turned suddenly unfavorable. Several 10s are obviously in play on the table and no longer available. Accordingly, the 8 vs. 6 no longer calls for doubling but drawing.

On the other hand, imagine that an unfavorable minus-4 deck runs out during a round and is reshuffled, leaving cards on the table in play. All these cards must total plus 8, leaving a favorable, 10-rich partial deck.

If you will experiment a bit with a deck of cards, you can readily appreciate the significance of the reverse point count. In summary, an unfavorable point count will suddenly indicate a favorable deck if a reshuffle occurs in the midst of a round—with cards remaining in play. Conversely, a favorable count will indicate an unfavorable deck under similar conditions.

Often, of course, the reverse point count will be only approximate, as some unseen cards may have been ignored in the previous count. But a reasonable approximation is better than no information at all. It is vitally important to realize that when a shuffle occurs and you still have a hand in play, the significance of the point count is essentially opposite of what it was before the shuffle.

On rare occasions, some further practical use can be made of this phenomenon if you will *anticipate* that the count is about to reverse—that is, that the deck is about to run out. Circumstances can occur when you might play a hand differently if you realize that the dealer will be unable to make his draw before shuffling. It would be highly complicated and impractical to attempt an examination of all conceivable modifications of strategy that might be indicated. The situations I have in mind do not occur often. But when some highly aggressive strategy is based in large part upon a strong possibility that the dealer will break, you may want to forego the maneuver if you see that the available cards will be used before he can draw.

The highly obvious situation of this type can easily be illustrated. Suppose other players are to your left (for some reason you have taken a seat farther from third base than usual). Suppose also that the temporizing point count shows the uncounted deck to be highly 10-rich, you hold a pair of 10s, and the dealer shows a 5. The situation is one in which you would consider splitting the 10s. But suppose very few cards remain. You would have to take some of these if you split. Also, you do not know whether the players to your left may draw some. You recognize that if you split, the deck may run out before the dealer draws. Thus, the point count will reverse, and the dealer will be able to draw from the 10-poor reshuffled discards. His chance of breaking will be much reduced. In a situation like this, you may decide to forego the split and stand with your 20.

I can mention parenthetically that the preceding example also shows another reason why you should prefer to play near third base—or at an uncrowded table. If no one can draw between you and the dealer, you can judge much better whether the unplayed deck will hold out until the round is completed.

9

The Separate
Count of Aces

THIS system of playing Twenty-One involves many approximations. The one leading to the greatest inaccuracy involves an inherent defect in a 10-count system —the treating of all non-10s alike in the count. It is necessary to do this for the accuracy of the strategy changes and for intelligent insurance betting. And it is, of course, to the player's advantage, for purposes of varying his bets, to have *most* ranks of the non-10s out of the deck, although the precise degree of advantage varies between the ranks. The Ace is the one notable exception;* each Ace that is missing from the remaining deck is to the player's disadvantage.

Thus, for purposes of deciding the size bet to make, it is immensely helpful to know whether the unplayed deck contains an abnormally large or small proportion of Aces. The exact influence this proportion will have on the prospects for

---

*The 9 is also an exception but a minor one; we do not bother with it in our system.

winning a hand varies slightly with the rules in force. Various authors have differed slightly in calculating or estimating this influence. Under any circumstance, however, after all Aces are gone from the undealt deck, the casino has an advantage substantially more than 3 percent greater than the ratio of 10s to non-10s would otherwise indicate. On the more pleasant side, if twice as many Aces remain as normal, the *player* has an advantage between 3 percent and 4 percent greater than the 10/X ratio would indicate. Thus, if the deck is half played but no Aces have yet appeared, this latter situation will exist. Similarly, if only one-fourth of the deck remains, and the dealer does not shuffle, two Aces remaining will be twice as many as normal. And if only one-fourth remains and still contains all four Aces, the player's advantage will be exceptionally good provided the point count is anywhere near favorable.

Clearly, the criteria for changing the size of bets, as indicated by the point count, should be modified when the Ace count is abnormal. Extreme precision is difficult under the pressure of casino play. In other books it is common to find the suggestion merely to "lean" in one direction or another in allowing the Ace count to influence the size of bets. Nevertheless, with our point-count method, it is rather easy to achieve a fairly close correlation between the Ace ratio and the point count. Three rules of thumb cover reasonably well most circumstances in which the Ace count should have a *highly* important influence on betting strategy.

First, at any time after a round of hands has been dealt, and another will be dealt before shuffling, a bet larger than minimum should be made if: (a) *no* Ace has yet appeared, and (b) the point count is anything above zero.

Second, if all the Aces have been played, bets should be minimal unless the point count reaches *above* plus 8.

Third, if three of the Aces appear on the first round (or the first two rounds at an uncrowded table), the bet on the next hand should be minimal unless the point count is above plus 8.*

These three rules of thumb are approximations only, but they can be very useful. The first is highly logical. As the undealt deck becomes smaller, point counts between zero and plus 4 become increasingly less favorable; but the ratio of Aces to non-Aces will be greater to compensate for this disadvantage if all four remain in the deck. For the time being, bear in mind that the appearance of a single Ace invalidates this rule of thumb. If any Aces are out of the undealt deck, plus 4, as usual, should be regarded as the "point of departure" for increasing the size of bets (or even more than plus 4 if the conditions of the second or third rules are present). Later I will explain a slight modification.

The second and third rules are a bit less precise than the first, but their principle is obvious: if the deck is Ace-poor, somewhat more is needed, in terms of point count, than the usual plus 4 for increasing the size of bets.

This discussion assumes that the reader is already comfortable in keeping the point count, varying his bets accordingly, and playing proper strategy in view of the temporizing count. I have postponed it until now because the added chore of taking and using the separate Ace count will be an undue burden and will probably decrease efficiency in the other elements of play unless they are mastered first. Also, in most excursions through the deck, about one Ace will remain for each one-fourth deck remaining to be dealt; thus the Ace count will not affect your betting on the majority of hands. If

---

*For purposes of the third rule of thumb, return essentially to normal betting strategy on hands subsequent to the next one, or subsequent to the next two or so at an uncrowded table. But eventually you will want to bear in mind the refinements suggested at the end of this chapter.

anything in previous chapters (with the possible exception of the rarer adjustments for splitting pairs) is uncertain in your mind or causes hesitation in your play, I recommend further review and practice before you attempt to superimpose the separate Ace count upon the point count. This is a valuable tool for your assault on the casinos, and I regard it as an integral part of the system.

Learning to Count Aces

I had some difficulty at first in learning to keep the Ace count. Without this added mental chore, a successful Twenty-One player must employ the following armamentarium:

1. Know the game (Chapter 1).
2. Play basic strategy automatically (Chapter 2).
3. Keep the point count (Chapters 3 and 5).
4. Vary bets according to the count (Chapter 3, etc).
5. Take the temporizing count if indicated (Chapter 5).
6. Play the hand properly as indicated by the point count (Chapters 2, 4, 6, 7, and 8).
7. Try to hide what he is doing from the dealer, the pit boss, and their supervisors.
8. Make minor adjustments according to the rules and customs of the casino he is in.
9. Do everything very fast.

When I began to add the Ace count to all these requirements, it seemed too much. At first I tried to invent memory devices (mental use of fingers, toes, position of my foot, etc), but all that was silly. I was already (mentally and silently, of course) keeping the point count thus: "plus 1, minus 2, plus 2, minus 1, plus 4, plus 7," etc., as indicated. It suddenly was quite easy to add, each time an Ace appeared, "and 1," "and 2," "and 3," "and out." *Out* indicated that all Aces had been played. When the deck is freshly shuffled, the point count is, of course, zero, and I would begin "even and 0." As cards were played, I would mentally recite the point count to myself, adding "and 0," until an Ace appeared. Then, the count would be, "[Point count] and 1." And later, "[Point count] and 2."

You may want to devise your own memory device for keeping the separate Ace count. But I will illustrate mine briefly (hole cards underlined):

Deck just shuffled (count "even and 0") in a head-on game.
Dealer's hand—5,10,4.
My hand—9,6,5.
   (Count "plus 3 and 0"; increase bet.)
Dealer's hand—10,4,8 (bust).
My hand—9,6.
   (Count changes to "plus 5 and 0"; increase bet.)
Dealer's hand—10,10.
My hand—Ace,10 (blackjack).
   (Count changes to "even and 1"; decrease bet.)
Dealer's hand—10,7.
My hand—10,2,10 (bust).
   (Count changes to "minus 4 and 1"; continue to bet small.)
Dealer's hand—2,8,4,2,3.
My hand—7,6,2,3.
   (Count changes to "plus 5 and 1"; increase bet.)
Dealer's hand—10,5,9 (bust).
My hand—Ace,6,3 (I have doubled down).
   (Count changes to "plus 8 and 2"; increase bet.)
Dealer's hand—9,10.

My hand(s)—Ace,10; Ace,10 (I have split the Aces.)
(Count changes to "plus 5 and out"; decrease bet, despite the normally favorable count, as all Aces are gone.)

Refinements

Please bear in mind that the separate count of Aces ordinarily does not affect the play of the hands according to the strategy dictated by the point count. It is used only to modify betting tactics when the deck is abnormally Ace-rich or Ace-poor.

I should acknowledge a possible minor exception to these statements. The point count may occasionally reflect that a decision of whether to double down is borderline—virtually a toss-up. In such a circumstance, if my hand is, say, a 10 or 9, I may decide to double if the deck is highly Ace-rich and not to double if it is Ace-poor. If my hand is 11, the criteria are reversed because drawing an Ace would turn the hand into an unwanted 12. But I do not employ these refinements unless the situation is such that I am otherwise having trouble in deciding whether to double.

Once you have mastered the three rules of thumb given earlier in this chapter, you will have no trouble refining the betting strategy slightly more when the deck is just moderately Ace-poor. For example, if two Aces have appeared and the deck is clearly less than half played, or if three have appeared and the deck is clearly less than three-fourths played, you would want at least *something* above plus 4 in point count before increasing bets. But be careful not to exaggerate the influence of these situations. The deck is *seriously* Ace-poor only when all are gone or when three are gone with most of the deck remaining to be played—the circumstances for which I devised the second and third rules of thumb. With the deck only moderately Ace-poor, one or two points above plus 4 are enough to compensate for the deficiency.

After you become comfortable in using the Ace count, the second rule of thumb can be reduced to fair precision. When all Aces have been played, a point count moderately above that indicating the "excellent" deck of Chapter 7 is needed before increasing bets above minimum. Thus, a count of plus 10 is required very early in the deck, but plus 8 is enough late* in the deck.

The first rule of thumb, which applies to an Ace-rich deck, may be modified slightly when half or more of the deck has been dealt but enough cards remain for another round. Then a larger bet may be made at point-count zero or above even if one Ace (but only one) is out of the remaining deck. And if *no* Ace has yet appeared, a larger bet may be made a couple of points *below* zero! Although a zero point count late through the deck is much more unfavorable than it is earlier, a *highly* Ace-rich deck with few cards remaining will compensate even to greater degree.

The enormous influence of a *very* Ace-rich deck can be dramatized by considering the player's advantage with a plus-4 count and only one-fourth of the deck remaining, assuming he is sitting at an uncrowded table at which another full round of hands can be dealt. If all four Aces remain, the player has an advantage of about 11 percent, as contrasted with the usual 1 percent at plus 4. The situation is better than playing with a hypothetical 52-card deck in which 16 of the non-10s are Aces instead of only four! If three Aces remain in a quarter deck still to be dealt, the player has an advantage of about 8 percent with the point count plus 4. Clearly, bets should be large in these circumstances.

---

*For an estimate of the degree of deck depletion, glance at the discards in the return tray; if no tray is used, see the footnote page 41.

10

The Casino:
What Every Expert
Needs to Know

For the player of basic strategy, Twenty-One is the best gambling "buy" in Nevada. And for the player who can skillfully case the deck, the game offers the only opportunity in the casino to play against the house and have a statistical probability of winning. As noted in the Introduction, some other games (craps, for example) offer a variety of bets, involving greatly different house odds, from which a player may choose. But even the knowledgeable player can do no better than to select bets at craps that give a low house percentage (in the neighborhood of 1 percent) and avoid the sucker bets that almost assure early bankruptcy. Some other games (roulette is one) offer a wide range of pay-off propositions, but all entail exactly the same house odds (greater than 5 percent against the player at roulette), and no knowledge whatever can lessen these formidable odds. One popular game, keno, offers a tempting possibility of winning a small fortune for a minor investment, but the chance of doing so is infinitesimal, and the house take on this greedy game is formidable (around 20 percent). A few card games, such as poker, do offer the player the opportunity to use judgment and thus to outplay his opponents, but in these the game is against other players, with the casino dealer merely acting as broker and exacting a fee or a percentage from the winning pots. The house cut is so large that a reasonable result is to have every player at the table eventually losing, with the casino ending as the only one with a profit. This feature makes a substantial win difficult, although poker can be an entertaining diversion. The slot machines, with their inexorable and usually high house take, should be labeled, "For Amusement Only," and anyone who plays them very long or for any other purpose will find that his only "amusement" will be in seeing his money disappear. In greater or lesser degree, all the other casino games, of which there are many (baccarat, chuck-a-luck, the money wheel, the big six) exact a percentage of each bet, on the average, from the player. In the long run—and often in the short run—this percentage cannot be overcome.

Yet I would not advise the occasional visitor to Nevada to abstain completely from a bit of excitement in trying his luck at a few of these games. I occasionally throw a few nickels into the slots. Since I know the fairly reasonable bets that can be made on the dice table, I sometimes gamble a few dollars there. I may even waste a bit at roulette or (in some ways worse) take a small flier at keno. After all, Las Vegas is a playground. The fabulous entertainment, the gourmet food, the wonderful climate on the beautiful desert—all blend in that city without clocks to lead to a bit of frivolity.

But when I gamble at craps, poker, or whatever, I know I am *buying* my gambling, so I do it very infrequently. For there is always Twenty-One. And the game of Twenty-One is why this book is written.

How the Game is Run

The management of a large casino is both elaborate and orderly. Tables for the major games, such as Twenty-One, tend to be clustered around some central area, and groups of tables are supervised by "pit bosses."

The dealers and pit bosses ordinarily work eight-hour shifts, to make up three shifts per day (most casinos in Nevada do not close). During the shifts, of course, the personnel have regular rest periods. Dealers, for example, are commonly assigned to a particular table, and relief dealers will rotate from table to table on a prescribed schedule.

Frequent inventories are made of the turnover of money at each table. Play is suspended for a minute or two when the casino supervisory and security personnel visit a table to collect the accumulated cash and to keep the dealer's supply of chips at a satisfactory level.

Casinos vary somewhat in their degree of solicitude for the customers, but all provide free drinks, cigarettes, and other major or minor courtesies. The customer (player) usually does not even have to ask for these things, as they will be offered constantly.

A modern casino is the exception to the platitude that you can be alone in a crowd. In addition to the pit bosses, other personnel keep unobtrusive but constant watch over the proceedings. Devices such as two-way mirrors, perhaps with magnification, provide vantage points for close scrutiny. Observers are not necessarily behind these mirrors at all times, but they can readily be stationed there if anything suspicious develops on the casino floor. Security measures in a large casino are extensive, and personnel observe everything: players, dealers, pit bosses, one another, everything! You may even be on a hidden camera when you play.

Money Management

The proper management of money is as necessary for success at Twenty-One as any other of the principles presented in this book. The subject involves several important questions. How much money do you need when you begin to play? How much can you reasonably expect to win? How should you size your individual bets? How should you appraise certain popular betting schemes, or "systems"? Should "luck" influence your play?

Basically, the sizing of bets involves a rather simple matter: they should be large when the deck is favorable and small otherwise. However, the tactics of varying bets to take advantage of a favorable deck must be tempered to avoid pressing the casino into adopting measures that compromise successful play. But another important requirement for probable success is to manage your total capital so that you will not be wiped out by a temporary run of bad luck.

In the first place, you should *never* gamble with money you cannot afford to lose. Chance fluctuations in the run of the cards can overcome a statistical advantage, and there is no absolute guarantee of winning. Besides the obvious folly of risking money that is needed for something else, doing so compounds the danger by leading to bad play. It can affect judgment in various harmful ways. At best, mental concern about the money on the table is distracting and induces errors. At worst, some players, after a series of losses, abandon sound play and begin foolish, wild gambles in the hope of being suddenly lucky. Others, while not yielding to such harmful impulses, may nevertheless be intimidated into overcaution and fail to press advantages when they appear—fail to increase bets properly or fail to split or double down when indicated. For best prospects, the player ordinarily should allocate a specific sum of gambling capital that he can well afford to lose and, for practical purposes, consider it already spent.

Initial Capital

The player's capital should be large enough to provide a comfortable reserve in case of early losses. To state the same thing differently, the average single bet should be sufficiently small that the player can, for a while if necessary, lose a substantial number of individual hands exceeding the number he wins without depleting his capital.

If fortune is particularly unkind and this gambling capital is lost or reduced to an uncomfortably small reserve, the question of whether to replenish must be answered by each individual player. The decision should be made unemotionally, and the capital should not be replenished with money that is needed for something else. If the player plans to continue the game (and why not?) and does not want to replenish his funds, he should reduce his single bets or temporarily abstain until his overall personal finances again show a bit of surplus.

It is difficult to state a precise amount of gambling capital that a player ideally should set aside. The matter involves the mathematical problem of "gambler's ruin"—the chance of losing all of a stated sum of money, given a known statistical advantage or disadvantage on each bet, while attempting to win a stated sum. Mathematicians have calculated such chances with precision, given exact information as to percent advantages and size of bets. However, the play of Twenty-One does not lend itself to this precision in calculating the chance of gambler's ruin. The variation of individual bets, the uncertainties in how frequently the dealers will shuffle the deck, rule variations between casinos, and other factors prevent a knowledge of the exact average percent advantage the player will have. With the method given in this book, including intelligent variation of bets and standard Las Vegas rules, I roughly estimate the overall advantage as about 2 percent. The more liberal rules of a few casinos increase it slightly, but the restrictions of standard Reno rules decrease it more. Under *worst* Reno rules (no insurance, no surrender, and doubling restricted to 10 and 11), the advantage is probably less than 1½ percent. The percent advantage could be increased considerably if bets in favorable situations could be increased substantially more than I generally suggest, but attempts to employ such tactics are very likely to induce the dealer to shuffle early. A fairly large amount of capital is needed, in relation to the size of bets, to cushion against a series of losses and thus provide a high probability of winning eventually.

Assuming the 2 percent advantage, suppose you plan to make $5 to $20 bets, with your average bet about $10. If you start with $500 capital, your prospects of winning will be very good; nevertheless, there *is* about one chance in seven or eight that you will instead lose the $500 in a prolonged period of play. On the other hand, if you start with $1,000, it is *very* unlikely that you will lose your stake. The odds are about 40 or 50 to one that you will eventually win instead. But if you have only $100 or even $200 to lose, your prospects of winning in prolonged play, before chance fluctuations in the run of the cards demolish your capital, are actually *less* than even! In fact, with only $100, it is *highly* improbable that you will eventually win. In other words, if you play indefinitely, there is the great probability that at *some* point in time you will find yourself $100 behind, despite an average 2 percent advantage on the individual hands. If you have much less than $500, it may be better to use dollar chips and bet $1 to $4 or $2 to $8. In northern Nevada, where most casinos have less favorable rules, you should shade the requirement for initial capital upward slightly to have a really high probability of success.

This discussion will have different application to different people. It may mean little to the independently wealthy player, as his capital reserve can be about as much as he wishes. The point is that the more *units* of gambling capital a player can afford to lose, the better his chances are of winning. But even a player with almost unlimited resources should maintain some orderliness in managing his gambling finances. If he finds he loses frequently and continues to do so over a long period of time, he should reassess his game in conjunction with the method presented in this book. Perhaps he is doing something wrong.

Of course, a player's *goal* can make one system of money management reasonable even though it would be highly risky with a different goal. A rather small amount of capital is satisfactory if a player is willing to *accept* a high risk of early ruin. For example, a player living in the vicinity of the casinos can play successfully with relatively little capital reserve at a given time. (But he should remember that I am speaking of *gambling* capital. He must exercise self-discipline to avoid risking money he needs for other purposes.) If he loses what he initially allots to play, he can conveniently return when he can *afford* another allotment. Thus, his true gambling capital is really the total of a series of allotments, and eventually he should come out ahead, using my system.

But one thing is definite. Beginning with only a small number of betting units, a player runs a considerable risk of losing them, because an early run of misfortune can wipe him out. Thus, this discussion has its greatest application to an out-of-state visitor who wishes to play frequently over a period of several days and have good prospects of beating the game. I recommend that, in addition to what he will need for expenses, he should have a gambling capital at least 100 times his average bet. With a realistic system of varying bets, this will mean about 200 times his *minimum* bet. A bit more than this amount is desirable, to assure equanimity.*

Before leaving the subject, I offer one further word of advice: unless money means little to you, I suggest that you bet rather small units until you have tested yourself not only in practice but in actual casino play. If you plan to play for larger amounts, wait until you are sure you can play the system comfortably, confidently, and with few mistakes. It is unwise, however, to prolong unduly this period of "breaking in" to casino play. Your best prospects for winning come when you are a stranger to the casino personnel. Thus, if you make yourself too well known in too many casinos before you decide to graduate to heavy betting, you will squander much of the desirable elment of anonymity.

Expected Yield

I am sure you will readily understand that you can never predict your winnings (or losses) over a short period of time. Fluctuations of chance are inherent to gambling. Nevertheless, with an average advantage of about 2 percent, you can make a reasonable estimate of your *probable* winnings over a period of prolonged play. To do so, you need only to know approximately the expected "action"—the total amount of all your bets.

You can expect to average playing about 100 hands an hour. The exact number at any one session will naturally vary according to the number of players present and the speed of

---

*I recommend Allan Wilson's book[7] for a readily understandable discussion of gambler's ruin. It will add much insight to the suggestions I have made in this section.

the dealer. At a full table, 70 or 75 hands an hour seem about average. If you can play a head-on game with a fast dealer, you can approach 200 hands an hour. Moderately crowded tables will, of course, yield something in between. All estimates take into consideration the delays of the dealer's shuffling, making change, and interrupting the game briefly for other purposes.

Thus, you can easily see that your statistical expectation of probable gain in one hour is about twice your average bet per individual hand. At a glance, this may seem small. If, for example, your average bet is $10, your action will average about $1,000 per hour.* Thus, over the very long run, your expectation is only about $20 an hour.* If this is not very impressive, I will remind you that enjoyment of the game and the excitement of winning can be something of a reward in themselves. Also, $100 a day for about five hours' pleasant endeavor is not really a bad goal.

But if it seems small, consider the prospects of using $25 chips with an average bet of $50. Your reasonable expectation, in the long run, is about $100 an hour. As explained previously, however, a program of bets of this size will require several thousand dollars in reserve capital to give fairly safe protection against gambler's ruin.

One additional thing, which may be unnecessary to mention: gambling winnings are taxable.

Bet Variation with a View to Camouflage

If the dealer does not already know you case the deck, you should do everything practicable to hide the fact from him. This will help to avoid some of the casino countertactics to be

---

*Really a bit more if your average *initial* bet is $10, as doubling down, splitting pairs, and taking insurance will add some. But I am attempting here to give only a rough and slightly conservative guide to the matter discussed.

discussed in the next section. Sometimes the casino personnel may suspect you of casing but may not be sure. Let them remain in doubt.

Obviously, you should not advertise your counting of cards by peering with undue enthusiasm at each one. It is perfectly natural for your casual gaze to wander along following the cards as they are exposed. Be nonchalant. A good poker face can hide the fact that your brain is working intensely.

Except for avoiding obvious giveaways, the most important technique of camouflage is proper betting tactics. The cornerstone of good betting tactics is to make apparently natural variations. There should be no obvious clues to alert the dealer that your larger bets coincide with a favorable deck.

A method I sometimes use is to start with one chip and to continue to bet one if the deck remains neutral or becomes unfavorable. Whenever the deck turns favorable, I bet two. The next time, if the deck is still favorable, I bet three or four. Whenever the deck becomes neutral again or unfavorable, I go back to one chip.

The innocuous appearance of this scheme is discussed in Chapter 3. It is very common for a gambler to let a winning bet "ride," or to "double-up and catch-up" after losing. This action explains increases from one chip to two and from two to four. It induces no excitement to reduce from a high bet to a minimal one, but it is suspicious to increase suddenly from a low bet to a much higher one. I almost never increase from one to four and not too often from one to three.

A slightly different scheme can be used, often to greater advantage. Start with two chips after the deck is freshly shuffled. Reduce to one on the next hand unless the deck has turned favorable, but increase to four if it *has* turned favorable. This plan is especially good at a crowded table. When six or seven players are present, two rounds of hands will usually deplete the deck so much that the dealer will shuffle. It often is virtually predictable that a dealer will shuffle after the second round. Thus, your opportunities to make four-chip bets in favorable situations will depend on two-chip initial bets if you follow my advice against precipitous increases. The initial two-chip bet is also quite acceptable at an uncrowded table; it is somewhat more aggressive than the initial one-chip bet and eventually will get more money into play. This result, of course, is generally desirable for a winning player if, of course, the large bets are compatible with his capital.

Both schemes just discussed have assumed a one-chip minimum bet and a four-chip maximum. However, many players may want to bet larger amounts than this will allow with $5 chips, yet they feel reluctant to go as high as a $25 minimum. You can, of course, vary from two to eight chips or from three to twelve. But if you *are* making frequent bets of, say, $40 or $60, do not be tempted to reduce to only $5 in unfavorable situations—or at least not often. Such a wide variation by an obviously knowledgeable player is practically an advertisement that he is casing.

Even with a betting scheme that allays suspicion, do not follow it *too* rigidly—it may give you away. If you are varying from one to four chips and your initial bet after shuffling is ordinarily two, sometimes make it one; if it is one, sometimes make it two. Sometimes bet three instead of four, particularly after a loss of two, in which case the change will not involve drawing back any chips that were won. If you are varying from two to eight chips, sometime after the shuffle make your initial bet three and sometimes two or four. But ordinarily avoid camouflaging variations when the deck is unfavorable; make only your minimum bet, whatever that may be.

I should mention that any betting system involving large stacks of chips by an obviously skilled player has a slight fundamental disadvantage. For psychological reasons, even though you never bet less than $10 or $15, eight or twelve $5 chips on a hand may excite a dealer more than $100 if you were playing exclusively with $25 chips. It may be better not to attempt the four-fold fluctuation between minimum and maximum. Vary from two or three chips to six or seven, with enough apparent erraticism to seem capricious.

Occasionally, the denomination of chips will afford a convenient stratagem for making a large bet in a highly favorable situation without causing excitement. For example, if you are betting $5 chips and have been losing temporarily, you may find that only $25 denominations remain in your stack. The dealer, of course, will give you change if you wish. But if the deck is highly favorable, you may decide on an apparent "sudden impulse" to bet the entire larger chip.

If a seat beside you is vacant, it presents a readily available opportunity to increase the "action" with relatively low individual bets. You can play two hands. (If you wish, you can even play three if enough adjacent spots are open.) In playing two hands, you may be required to bet at least twice the usual table minimum on one or both. This requirement is fairly routine at low-minimum tables, but it is likely to be ignored at higher-minimum tables.

Basically, playing two hands is not quite as statistically advantageous as betting the entire sum on one hand. After the first hand is played, the bet on the second would sometimes be different if it were not already committed. Nevertheless, the overall effect is minor, and dividing moderately large bets into two smaller ones can provide excellent camouflage: two bets of $20 each just do not excite the dealer as much as one stack of eight $5 chips. Also, playing two hands, you will always have the advantage of knowing the hole cards of the first hand

when you play the second. (Except when the dealer shows an
Ace and offers insurance, you are usually asked not to look at
your second hand until you have finished playing your first.)

Wouldn't it be nice to play two hands every time the point
count turned favorable, and one otherwise? Unfortunately,
the casinos are not so stupid as to put up with that. You will
generally be asked not to vary unduly between playing one,
two, or three hands.

If possible, you should make some attempt to anticipate
when the dealer will shuffle so that you can avoid being
caught with a large bet out (because of a favorable deck) and
suddenly find the dealer shuffling to return the deck to
neutral.

Often, the size of the remaining deck and the dealer's previous habits will make it evident that he will not shuffle. At
other times, for the same reasons, you will be certain that he
will. When you are not sure, you may be able to fumble with
your chips for a moment in deciding the size of your next bet
(avoid doing this too often), casually talk to a friendly neigh-
bor, or be distracted by the cocktail waitress. But in general,
I suggest an intermediate bet when you *must* commit yourself
before the dealer has indicated, in one way or another,
whether he will shuffle. Of course, this problem is not present
when the deck is unfavorable or neutral; then your bet will
routinely be the minimum.

After you have placed your bet, you are allowed to retract
it before any cards are dealt the next hand, but the case-
down player who exercises this option on the obvious basis
that the dealer has decided to shuffle is a clear giveaway. I
suggest that if you fail to anticipate a shuffle and have made a
large bet, *leave it*. After all, with a neutral, freshly shuffled
deck, the odds are practically even anyway. And the subse-

quent temporizing count may give you a clue to how to play the hand to advantage.

Sometimes, a dealer may deliberately wait until you have placed your bet and then shuffle. If he does this more than a time or two, he probably knows or at least suspects that you are casing the deck. In this circumstance, when you see the dealer waiting and the deck is favorable, make only your minimum bet. Eventually, test him when the deck is neutral or slightly unfavorable: when he waits, make a larger bet. If he shuffles then, stay with that dealer as long as you can. Continue to repeat the same tactics.

Finally, regardless of any betting tactics you are using, one important ploy applies: when you have been paid for a win, *do not touch your money until you have decided the amount of your next bet.* For example, if the dealer pays you in turn for a win but still must settle two or three other bets, you often will not know whether to bet large or small on the next round until the other players' cards are exposed and counted. Simply leave all the money on the spot until you do know. Then reach out and either retract part or stack it all together for the next round. This creates far less suspicion that you are basing your decision on the cards you see than if you withdraw the chips and later decide how many to put back. Certainly you should not make some tentative decision on the size of the bet and then obviously change your mind after seeing additional cards.

There is a single exception to the practice of not touching the money until the next bet is decided. When I am paid early for a blackjack at a crowded table, I *do* retract *all* of the money immediately. A considerable waiting period will remain until the round is completed and all other bets are settled. It does not appear natural to leave the money out for that length of time and then decide not to bet it all when the dealer is ready for another round.

Progressive Betting "Systems"

It is fortunate for the expert that most Twenty-One players employ some variation in the size of their bets from hand to hand. This keeps the expert's bet variation from necessarily attracting attention right away. It makes little difference to us whether, in sizing bets, the other players use superstitious criteria, pure whim, or some pseudo-scientific "system" based upon the notion that some scheme of bet variation *per se* can insure success. We only need to be aware of such practices in order to avoid being tempted into following them.

Untold numbers of mathematically naive gamblers have attempted to devise stratagems designed to overcome the house odds merely through sizing bets according to some sequence based on the outcome of previous betting transactions. The commonest and simplest of these is the classic *martingale*. Whether recognized by name or not, the martingale has probably occurred to almost everyone who has devoted any thought to gambling. It involves bets with even-money payoffs, and it requires doubling the bet after every loss and returning to the amount of the first bet after every win. Thus, if a player bets one unit and loses, he would next bet two units. If he loses again, he would bet four. Next time eight. And so forth, until he wins, recouping prior losses plus winning one unit. After every win, the next bet is routinely one unit, and a new series begins. Theoretically, a losing sequence cannot continue forever, and the player must win eventually.

The martingale or some variation thereof is often attempted with the even-money bets at roulette, such as red or black or even or odd. It can similarly be played with, say, the line bets at craps. Naturally, at roulette, craps, or baccarat the casino has a statistical advantage on each wager. But the theory holds that such odds can be overcome by the fact that red cannot recur forever on the roulette wheel—the "bank" cannot win every time at baccarat. Because of the intrusion of doubling-down and pair-splitting situations, the martingale is not completely applicable to Twenty-One. But a devotee of the system can ordinarily invent some adaptation to compensate for that problem.

The entire notion of the martingale reeks with practical absurdities. The most readily evident in a casino game is the house limit. Consider, for example, a roulette game at which a range of bets from $1 to $500 can be made on black. If a player's basic bet is $1, he will be unable fully to double his bet whenever a series of losses brings his bet to $256 and he then loses that. Such a situation will develop at any time he has nine losses in a row. The best he can do (making loose use of the term *best*) is to bet $500 on the next turn. If he loses *that*, his martingale series ends in a large loss.

Suppose, just for argument, that he attempted to continue the series by having partners stationed about to make additional bets of up to $500 each when indicated. A mere two additional turns would require four partners if the series were continued in full. If these two turns were lost, all the fun would be over.

Thus, an unrestricted martingale is not possible under normal casino conditions. But even if a casino made it possible by removing the limit, there must always be *some* limit to a player's capital. And after a long string of losses, the sums necessary to perpetuate the series become astronomical. To *guarantee* success, an *infinite* amount of money would be necessary—a requirement that could never be met.

The lure of the system, of course, is the fact that even if not impossible, it is very *unlikely* that, say, eight or ten losses will occur in a row at any given time. But even at coin tossing, where no house odds are involved and the chances of winning or losing are exactly even on each toss, ten losses in a row will occur in each 1,024 series. After beginning with $1, the bet on the tenth toss will require $512; to reach that sum, a total of $1,023 will have been bet in an effort to win $1! It is the paltry sum to be won that exposes the fallacy of the system. To win anything near the amount being risked, the player must continue to play many repeated series, and eventually the uncommon occurrence of ten or more losses in a row will occur.

In the coin-tossing example just given, the player at least has an even statistical chance. If he has the capital to continue doubling for ten losses, he has, on any series, one chance in 1,024 of losing his capital; but he has corresponding odds of 1,023 to 1 that he will win the dollar. Coin tossing, however, is not played in the casinos, and at a game like roulette, there is less than an even chance that black (or red) will appear on a spin; one time in 19, green will appear instead of either other color. Under circumstances like these, ten losses in a row will occur *much* more often than one in 1,024. Against that game the martingale must fail.

Many progressive betting schemes more elaborate than the martingale have been devised. But they generally involve some formula for increasing bets after losing and returning to some smaller amount after winning. They generally deceive the user in the same way as the martingale: the player usually *does* win at first. They have the common denominator that a loss is very unlikely on any one or any few series of bets. Beginning at any point in time, the probability is very·high that the user will accumulate at least some small amount of winnings and naively believe that he has found the road to fortune. He waxes enthusiastic until that long run of losses, improbable at any one time but inevitable eventually, brings a devastating loss. And a few players, of course, will be so unlucky as to have a ruinous run of losses almost immediately. It is perhaps merciful that they are spared the temporary illusion that they have discovered the gambler's nirvana.

Allan Wilson's book[7] contains a longer, readily understandable exposé of various progressive betting schemes. Also, *The Science of Chance*, by Horace C. Levinson,[14] examines this subject in even more detail. I will not belabor the matter further, as it represents essentially an academic digression from our subject. We merely increase our bets, within reason, when the point count is favorable.

Also, you may be amused now and then to see some player keeping elaborate and mystical records of each betting transaction. Such a person is probably trying to discern some recurring pattern of events that will allow him to predict a winning sequence. While probably futile, such behavior might make a grain of sense in attempting to detect a bias in a roulette wheel. But at Twenty-One, a player who does this does not understand the principle of independent trials: the outcome of one series of hands has no relationship to that of another (except, of course, as influenced by the play of cards in a given excursion through the deck).

This subject leads to the one of pure superstition to follow. An illustration is provided by a story once told me as true. It seems that a fellow had enough information about arithmetic to know that the chance is only one in 1,024 that heads will occur ten times in a row of coin tosses. He tossed until he observed nine straight heads. Then, he was willing to offer high odds that it would not occur again on the next toss! He thought the event was just about impossible.

The analysis of this man's fallacy is simple. At the beginning the chance was only one in 512 that heads would occur the first *nine* times. But at the tenth toss *those odds had already been overcome.* They were no longer relevant. The tenth toss was completely independent from the others; the chance for heads was exactly one in two, just as it had been for the first toss or for any other *one* toss.

The Superstition of "Hot" and "Cold"

Many people who intellectually understand the principles just discussed nevertheless take curious attitudes toward gambling.

Every gambler has periods of play in which luck is almost unbelievably good. At other times, it is deplorably bad. These episodes are usually called "hot" and "cold" streaks. They must not be misunderstood.

Once I was playing in a Strip casino, having indifferent success, when the dealer became talkative. He expounded on the many "bust" hands he had drawn earlier in the day. With an air of profoundness, he declared, "I've been in this business all my life. If just one time I could be on your side of the table and find a dealer as cold as I was this afternoon, I could retire."

The remaining inanity was predictable. "Why, I'd be betting $500 on every hand. I'd double down every time I couldn't break. I'd split every pair except tens. I'd absolutely get rich. I just hope that some day when I can play, I can run into a dealer having a streak like mine was then."

Just how this man would *know*, in the midst of a series of good fortune, that it would continue was not explained. In fact, while runs of luck definitely do occur, they can be appraised only in retrospect. Yet this fatuous dealer's monologue illustrated the most common and dangerous superstition among gamblers.

While some people learn from experience, gamblers often seem to be deceived by it. Every now and then, they do win for a while with uncommon frequency, begin to bet wildly, and continue to win for a while longer. They congratulate themselves on their cleverness. But just as often, after any series of wins, a series of losses will begin. After a few such losses, the type of gambler I am discussing will either quit or revert to small bets. Again he will feel highly pleased by his supposed expertise, although often just those few large bets will have obliterated the winnings of the several prior smaller bets.

The thing such gamblers forget is the many times they lose from the start. True, if they quit after a short period of losing, they will minimize their losses for any one session; but they will never know how often fortune would have changed immediately for the better. They also forget the many times when they win very briefly at the beginning but then promptly revert to losing.

On the average, any *overall* appraisal of the total winning and losing of players who think they can predict lucky and unlucky sequences, based upon prior sequences, will simply be reflected by the odds on the game. The player who limits his "cold streaks" to small losses and thinks he is waiting for a "hot streak" will normally have to endure a much larger number of those cold streaks, in one way or another, than the few sustained hot streaks that appear to provide a large win.

There are books, written in all seriousness, that offer the fatuous advice that a player should bet heavily when he is winning and small when he is losing. The advantage of such a procedure is obvious, but the advice is not stated quite accurately. If translated, it says: bet heavily *after* winning and small *after* losing. Reduced to these terms, such counsel has no substance, and it is totally inane for an expert Twenty-

One player. In summary, while "hot" and "cold" streaks do occur, the length of either is purely a matter of chance, and there is no way to predict how long either will last.

To avoid the appearance of contradicting myself, I should mention two minor ways that such streaks *can* alter your play in a reasonable manner. First, if you have either won or lost enough to change the size of your total capital substantially, the danger of gambler's ruin will be altered accordingly. This fact may sometimes lead you to make some adjustment in the overall size of your bets. Second, an undue pattern of losses *may* suggest at least the possibility of cheating (to be discussed later). However, these considerations really have nothing to do with the current discussion.

Do unsound gambling methods ever succeed? Naturally, through sheer luck, many brief contests are won against house odds. Otherwise, there would not be the bait to keep potentially losing players returning to the casinos. But what about the boasts of some people who claim to have won at length with progressive betting schemes, or who "always" win by betting heavily on "hot streaks?" What about the legends surrounding a few fabulous gamblers sufficiently lucky to win fortunes while defying statistical probabilities? Are any of these stories true? Undoubtedly, a few really are, and such phenomena can be explained mathematically. Let me illustrate with an example.

Imagine a lottery in which one winner will be drawn from a million numbers. The holder of any number obviously has only one chance in a million of winning. Such odds are formidable—statistically almost impossible against any individual. Yet *one* number will be drawn. Thus follows the absolute certainty that *one* participant in the lottery will be so lucky as to overcome one-million-to-one odds. If that person happened to have walked around his chair, rubbed seven rabbits' feet, and howled thirteen times at the moon, a new formula for success could become popular. Of course, we would never hear from any of the 999,999 who may have resorted to the unsuccessful strategy of nailing twenty-two horseshoes over the casino door on Halloween.

To summarize, there are two ways to win at casino gambling in the long run: be the lucky one person in a million or be an expert at Twenty-One. The choice is clear.

Casino Countertactics

I have mentioned a few of the countertactics the casinos can adopt to defend themselves against expert players. Unless a casino resorts to such measures as downright cheating or barring a player from the games, none of these tactics are fully effective, but they do tend to reduce the player's profits. Some casinos and some individual dealers adopt certain of the tactics routinely, just in case an unknown expert should be present. But the tactics are applied much more vigorously and frequently if one is known to be at the table.

Many casino personnel cannot recognize expert play when they see it, but they can recognize a steadily enlarging stack of chips by a winning player, and this may put them on their guard.

Individual dealers vary greatly, largely on the basis of their personalities, in their degree of concern about whether they win or lose against an individual player. Many could not care less; they do not pay their losses from their own pockets, and they receive no commissions from their winnings. Of course, they could not lose steadily and long against everyone without causing concern, but there is no real danger of this. Some dealers obviously like to see their customers win. (If for no other reason, their tips tend to be larger.) But the most benign dealer must take his orders from the pit boss, and when the pit boss tells him to go after a player, the dealer has no choice but to do so.

Cheating

I do not pretend to be an expert on cheating at cards in general or Twenty-One in particular. I do not know how commonly it occurs in the casinos of Nevada; they operate legally under the regulation of a state agency, which can bring drastic legal action against a casino that is caught. Collver's book would indicate that the practice is almost nonexistent. Those of Thorp and Wilson suggest that it is rampant. The authors present chilling revelations of their encounters with blatant cheating in Nevada during their pioneer studies of scientific Twenty-One. It should be noted, however, that their experiences occurred several years ago. Revere is perhaps best qualified to appraise current conditions. He confirms popular rumor that cheating is extremely uncommon in large, highly patronized casinos but much more common in very small, marginally operated places. One of my dealer-friends assured me that cheating does occur; he even warned me about specific shifts at specific casinos, although obviously I cannot repeat these allegations. (Practices can change, and I have some reason to think that his particular objects of concern have now been at least partly corrected.)

The fact that the Nevada State Gaming Control Board, which is the enforcement arm of the Nevada Gaming Commission, occasionally still closes a casino for cheating, basing its case on solid evidence, certainly suggests that the practice must go uncaught at other times—either because of lack of detection or lack of adequate evidence. On the other hand, if I were cheated most of the times I play, or even a substantial minority of the times, I could not win. And I do win. I am positive that nearly all of the games are honest. My advice to the reader is to be constantly aware of the possibility that he may come against a cheating dealer but not to be overly intimidated by suspicion. Perhaps you may never be cheated at all.*

Some of the hoary cheating methods do not lend themselves well to the modern Las Vegas games. Most traditional methods of deck stacking, besides being fundamentally difficult, are made particularly impractical by the necessity that the dealer pick up the cards in such order that he can deal the hands back in case of dispute. The custom of placing discards into a return tray instead of on the bottom of the deck eliminates the possibility of turning the deck over and redealing the same cards (a practice that an expert player would soon detect anyway). Most games in northern Nevada continue the practice of placing discards upside-down on the bottom of the deck. But here, too, if the procedure is done properly, the discarded hands are kept in order.

A crude chestnut of cheating at Twenty-One is to remove a few cards from the deck—say a few 10s, which are particularly valuable to the player. It seems almost inconceivable that a casino would try this today, yet one was caught doing so with a four-deck game fairly recently.

The danger of marked cards can be almost ignored. The casinos are very alert to the threat of *players* attempting to mark cards for their own benefit. But if a casino marked its cards, it would provide physical evidence of cheating—leading to much easier conviction in court. Equally cogent, the dealer could take no advantage of knowing the identity of a marked

---

* John Scarne's *Scarne on Cards* is highly recommended reading for anyone wishing a detailed discussion of card-cheating techniques. I should caution, however, that I do not endorse Scarne's advice about the play of Twenty-One.

card unless he combined the information with some manipulation—dealing seconds, for example. And a crook sufficiently
adept to deal seconds would surely develop an accompanying
skill at peeking at the top card without relying on markings.

The practice of peeking and dealing seconds is the cornerstone of card cheating. It is particularly applicable to
Twenty-One, and it is devastating. A skillful card mechanic
can look at the top card, retain it for future use if he desires,
and deal the second card in full view of everyone without
easy detection. Even other experts at card manipulation have
trouble in identifying second dealing with certainty.

The effect of this cheating maneuver can be appreciated
with a moment's reflection. If the dealer knows the top
card, he can deal it if he knows it will break the player's
hand—or if he thinks it will not help the player. He can
retain it for himself, dealing the second card to the player,
if he needs that top card for his own hand. If he knows the
top card will help the player, he can retain it and deal the
second. He does not have to know the second card; he will
gladly take a chance on the second card to avoid dealing the
known first card. When he draws to his own hand, he has a
choice of a known first card or an unknown second. His
choice is usually clear-cut.

Scarne and Collver provide pictorial illustrations of the
technique of peeking. With a practiced sleight of hand and a
fast glance, the dealer can look at the top card undetected.
And he can do so without such devices as tiny hidden
mirrors so often described in accounts of card cheating.
Most such devices would not be practical under the conditions of modern professional Twenty-One, but the expert
cheat, or "card mechanic," does not need them anyway.

I have played against dealers who were frivolously practicing their technique of peeking. With their friends (other

dealers) present as players, they would announce accurately what cards they and the players were about to draw. When I was more naive than now and a dealer told me I was about to break just before he hit me with another 10, I asked him how he knew the card. His answer was almost indignant: "I *looked* at it!" I am certain that this dealer did not cheat anyone at that session, but what about the next time—against someone else? If he practiced peeking so assiduously as to be an expert at it, a reasonable assumption is that he also would learn to deal seconds.

A traditional substitute for second dealing is the use of an anchor man. After identifying the top card, the dealer signals a confederate, usually sitting at third base, whether to draw or stand. The purpose is not ordinarily to help the hand of the confederate (anchor man) but rather to dispose of the top card or to retain it, whichever is advantageous to the dealer. I think it is unlikely that you will come against this crude practice in modern Twenty-One. For one thing, it lends itself readily to detection. To be very effective, the anchor man must play in a highly inconsistent and superficially irrational manner, since he draws or stands according to the dealer's instructions instead of the content of his own hand.

One of my friends, also an expert player, recently caught a dealer using a technique thus far not described in the discussions of cheating I have read. My friend detected that toward the end of the deck in which the burn card was placed under the deck, there would not be a single card present but several. I have mentioned previously the rapid, sleight-of-hand method with which dealers can burn the top card. This man was doing it repeatedly during the midst of the deal. My friend watched carefully. He had to play his hands while watching and thus only *saw* the man burn an extra card once. But that was enough. Always, about half a dozen cards were upside down at the bottom of the deck toward the end.

The possibilities of this cheating technique are intriguing. The dealer might just retire a few unknown cards to confuse the casedown player—a sort of early shuffle-up. Or he might peek and retire a few 10s and Aces from the deck— with devastating effect on any player. Carried to the ultimate, the dealer might peek, retain *or* burn the card, and deal seconds or firsts at his choice. Or, he might stack a couple of hands underneath and perform a turnover.

There is one additional cheating method for which you should be on the lookout. It is rather crude and requires less skill than most. A security guard I know in Reno revealed it to me, saying that he knew some of the dealers there used it. I do not know whether it has some jargonized name in the dealer's trade, but without much imagination I have titled it the *Reno shuffle*.

With the Reno shuffle, the dealer merely pushes an undue number of 10s and Aces to the top of the deck during the shuffle. Then, with the usual cut near the center of the deck, these cards end near the bottom. After dealing almost to them, the dealer reshuffles, and these cards, so desirable from the player's standpoint, are never quite reached.

Against the Reno shuffle the card-counting player is particularly misled. He will repeatedly find the deck with a high point count, yet he will never reap the benefits from the apparently favorable deck.

Eccentric cutting can *tend* to frustrate the Reno shuffle. Instead of cutting the deck near the center, the player can cut near the bottom—or occasionally just a few cards from the top. Obviously, however, no dealer engaged in the technique would really allow a player to take charge of the game in such manner. In addition to having exclusive control over when to shuffle, the dealer has the choice of which player is offered the deck to cut.

Lest you become overly concerned, I should mention that during my extensive play, I have not once been certain that the Reno shuffle was being used against me, and I have only been moderately suspicious a time or two. I merely advise you to be on guard against its possibility.

If you read extensively on cheating or listen to some card players, you will probably encounter an item of advice that is really inane when applied to professional Twenty-One. You will be cautioned to beware of a dealer who uses the "mechanic's grip." (The deck is held well back in the hand, and instead of all four fingers, only the last three are curled around the deck. The forefinger is wrapped around the leading edge; the thumb is on top near this edge.) That grip facilitates cheating manipulation. The problem is that if you avoid dealers who hold the cards in this manner, you can forget about playing casino Twenty-One. They *all* do it. I use the mechanic's grip when I deal cards, and I certainly do not cheat. After becoming accustomed to the grip, I simply found that the more common, amateurish method of holding the cards feels awkward.

I repeat that I do not know how many casinos allow or encourage cheating dealers. I wonder how often otherwise respectable casinos will ignore crooked employees who cheat for the house. But a plague on both players and management are the dealers who cheat for themselves, helping a confederate to win, and make up for the losses by cheating honest customers. The temptation to do this is strong. Thus, you should be delighted about the two-way mirrors, the pit bosses, the security personnel, and the State Gaming Control Board. Other parts of this section on casino countertactics will deal with less sordid measures that may be used against you.

Barring

If reasonable rules are in force, an honest casino has one and only one reliable measure to prevent an expert from beating it: to bar him from playing. Such extreme action is not taken commonly against players who are not too aggressively greedy and who do not conduct themselves in an obnoxious manner. Nevertheless, casinos do sometimes bar an obviously skillful card counter, particularly if he plays too often and for very high stakes.

Shuffle-Up

The cornerstone of casino countertactics is to shuffle the deck whenever the player would have an advantage on the next hand. It is fairly uncommon nowadays to find a dealer who routinely deals to the last card. (Virtually none deal the *very* last card.*) Many casinos instruct their dealers never to deal through the deck. This precaution is taken in case an expert should happen to be at the table; it deprives him of the highly lucrative deck compositions that often exist when only a few cards remain. However, most of a deck usually will be dealt before it is shuffled. This is adequate to provide the expert with enough favorable compositions to win, though not so rapidly as if the entire deck were routinely used.

If a player is recognized as an expert, or perhaps merely suspected by casino personnel who cannot reliably detect expert play, more frequent shuffling may commence. Casinos and individual personnel vary greatly in how soon they will

---

* I know of only one exceptional casino where *every* card is dealt.

spot good play and in how long they will tolerate it before commencing to shuffle up. Whether the player is winning— and how much—definitely exert an influence. The prosperity and general policy of the individual casino is a factor. Usually, the whole thing is a bit unpredictable; at times I have played my game profitably and relatively unimpeded for hours, whereas at others, shuffling began quite soon (maybe I was remembered from some time before). But after so long a time, especially if you are winning steadily, a pit boss will tell the dealer to shuffle very frequently. One jargonized term for this instruction is, "Break the deck."

I have seen pit bosses go so far as to tell dealers to break the deck after *every* hand. This is not too common; for one thing, it annoys the other customers at the table. But in my own case, at least, the dealer does not have to continue the practice long; I take it as a not-too-subtle invitation to leave—and do so.

I have occasionally encountered a dealer who would simply shuffle every time I increased my bet. As mentioned previously, such a technique can be used to your great advantage if the dealer is so incompetent that you can induce him to shuffle whenever *you* wish. At times, it is not the *dealer's* competence that is involved but that of the pit boss. Some of the most satisfying sessions I have played have occurred when a dealer blindly followed instructions to break the deck every time I increased. This literally allowed me to control the game.

Hiding Cards

Frequent shuffling alone, of course, does not preclude successful play—unless the deck is shuffled after every hand. The practice merely reduces effectiveness. Combined with other countertactics, it makes winning even more difficult.

The second most important of these, in terms of commonness and effectiveness, is the dealer's hiding of cards.

This subject is discussed in Chapter 5 in conjunction with instructions on counting and estimating by inference. It simply involves the dealer's going out of his way to avoid exposing the players' hole cards when bets are settled. This section should be reviewed for a description of the tactic—and for suggestions for countering it.

I know of one casino on the Strip that instructs its dealers routinely to follow this practice at every opportunity. It trains its apprentices ("break-in dealers") to hide every possible card. Elsewhere, you will merely encounter the technique sporadically.

Fast Play

With practice, you should be able to keep the point count and play accordingly as fast as any dealer can deal. Nevertheless, undue speed *can* induce mistakes now and then, and some dealers, as a countertactic against an expert, will adopt a frantic, jerky pace, which can be quite distracting. Typically, the technique will be combined with hiding cards and frequent shuffling. The dealing, adding of hands, settlements of bets, and even shuffles are at breakneck speed. Everything possible is done to rush the player. At head-on play, only a bare moment will be available for retracting any part of the bet after a win. When you lose a bet, the dealer will be annoyed unless you place your next bet quickly. (This is one time that you can slow him down, but you will have to readjust immediately to the whirlwind tempo.) The dealer will be nervously insistent that you decide promptly on whether to draw or stand, etc.; if you hold your cards a moment too long, he may "misinterpret" your action as a gesture that you want to draw and throw you another card. You can protest, of course, but the resulting arbitration, perhaps requiring the aid of the pit boss, is disconcerting. Dealers of this type *may* make an occasional "mistake" in adding up the hands or paying off; and at the whirlwind pace, you may not notice the "error" to correct it. One of these frenetic dealers actually hummed a little tune and performed a silly dance as he engaged in his hectic art.

Dealers Who Case

If you and I can case the deck, what would prevent a dealer from doing the same—and using the information to shuffle away decks favorable to the player or continue to deal decks that are unfavorable? Probably very little, although dealers who do so are uncommon.

Such practice would not deceive a case-down player; his casing presumably would coincide fairly well with that of the dealer if both were proficient. The expert would soon notice the "coincidences" in which unfavorable decks seemed to persist to the last card and favorable ones were promptly shuffled.

As a countertactic, casing by the dealer has only moderate usefulness. It could be used effectively until the expert player *did* catch on. More subtly, a really good dealer could case and merely "lean" toward shuffling or not shuffling; but this would only reduce the expert's advantage, not destroy it.

I will mention in passing that casing by the dealer would have a devastating effect upon the nonexpert. The good basic-strategy player would unwittingly be playing against a 10-poor deck most of the time. The innocent bad player would be largely deprived even of his small chance for a lucky winning streak. When viewed in this way, casing by the dealer is a subtle form of cheating. I cannot claim too strongly that a casing dealer cheats me because I also case and thus am even with him on that score. But he does cheat the ordinary player, who has a right to expect a random, unselected distribution of cards in the deck.

Some casino personnel may think that the *player* who cases is cheating. That idea is patent nonsense. The game of casino Twenty-One is formulated in a manner that offers the player options in his play and thus the use of whatever skill he has. The game also is formulated to give the dealer *no* options. The control of the dealer over when to shuffle does not disturb this arrangement if the time is elected in ignorance, but if the decision to shuffle is based upon a knowledgeable appraisal of the remaining deck, it is cheating. It has much the same effect as the practice of those casinos that have been caught removing a few cards from the deck. It seems unlikely to me that casing by the dealer would be interpreted as a violation of the law by the Gaming Control Board, but the possibility bears some thought.

When I say that rather few dealers case the deck, I mean in any systematic and sophisticated manner. One dealer told me that some casinos do ask their dealers to pay attention to Aces and to vary their shuffling tendencies accordingly near the end of the deck. However, I have not noticed the practice to be very commonly or skillfully employed. Even so, some dealers without the ability to case may nevertheless take impromptu advantage of an unusual deck composition that comes to their attention. For example, one of the most blatant premature shuffles I have seen occurred recently when I was watching a head-on game between a pathetically bad player and a very ordinary dealer. On the first hand after the shuffle, this player received two 5s, and the dealer showed some low card—a 3 or 4

I think. The player should have doubled down, but instead he drew, receiving another 5. With this hand, he should have stood, but he drew again—and got the fourth 5! The fact that he won with this foolishly acquired 20 is of no relevance to this anecdote. When the dealer eventually turned up the hand and saw all four 5s at once, he realized that the four worst cards in the deck, from the player's standpoint, would be missing on all subsequent deals. Ergo: he shuffled without dealing another single hand, against an obvious incompetent who had no idea of what was happening and who had practically no chance of beating him anyway. I am confident that this dealer could not case a deck. But virtually any dealer knows the importance of 5s, and when all four of them stared him in the face at once, he enthusiastically shuffled them back into the deck to deprive his naive opponent of a temporary, unrecognized advantage.

Shills

Casino personnel who sit at the tables and play among the customers will be the subject of a later section. As a legitimate countertactic against expert play, these people have only one function: to dilute the deck of cards so that favorable situations do not last as long.

Some casinos will not allow you to have a head-on game with the dealer. If you sit down at an empty table, or all the other players leave while you are playing, a shill will invariably appear to join you. There is no compelling reason to be disturbed by this practice. Some casinos use it, and some do not. If it annoys you too much, play elsewhere. But some very good casinos use it. I will defer detailed discussion of the functions of shills until later.

Amenities (Presence or Absence of)

All casinos are pleased to provide the players with free drinks. Smokers are given cigarettes of their choice and often fine cigars—ordinarily offered before they ask. Women are sometimes given a deck of used cards. It is common for players for fairly high stakes to be invited to dinner or to see a show. Various courtesies of this type are trivial matters to the casinos in view of the enormous exchange of money at the tables.

This discussion comes in the section on casino counter-tactics mostly because of the free cocktails. Too much alcohol will ruin judgment, and the casinos are only too pleased to serve all you want.

I would not presume to advise you on how much to drink while playing. That is your decision. But I warn you: if you drink enough to interfere with card counting; to influence the size of your bets; to make you uncertain of the correct ways to play your hands; to make you sleepy, inattentive, or frivolous; to lead you to guess and gamble when otherwise you would know proper play—you will certainly come away from a session cursing your impulse to play when drunk. Good play requires sobriety.

The case-down player must expect the red carpet of solicitude to be pulled back occasionally when the casino realizes that it is not fawning to another sucker but contesting an efficient opponent. The cigars may not be forthcoming. The cigarette smoker may be pointedly ignored when he asks for another pack. Various subtle discourtesies are possible. Ordinarily, a player who needs more chips during the play of a hand to split a pair or double down will be given a "marker" to be settled after the deal. With a case-down player, a surly pit boss may require the money in advance. The whole thing matters little, but I suggest that the prospective case-down player develop a "thick skin" and expect a few discourtesies—at least in certain casinos. If you can, look upon them as gestures of respect.

Some casinos may even see that the cocktail waitress ignores you. I cannot understand such stupidity; if they can get you drunk, they can probably beat you. Maybe *they* know that you know the same thing? I doubt this depth of conniving; the simple fact is that a lack of routine courtesies may induce you to take your business elsewhere.

Bad Rules

Rules variations are the subject of a later section in this chapter. However, it can be mentioned that the more options in play that are forbidden, the more difficult winning obviously becomes. The establishment of unfavorable rules by a casino is not precisely a countertactic in the sense that the term has been previously used, but it discourages the expert from playing. Fortunately, the practice discourages casual players too; thus, casinos usually find it inexpedient to alter the game too drastically and unfavorably from the norm (described in Chapter 1).

Player's Countertactics

Although casinos obviously control the type of game they will provide, including when and to what degree countertactics will be invoked, the player enjoys exclusive control over when and where he plays (unless a casino simply runs up the white flag and bars him from playing there at all). In general, the substantial measures available to the player for minimizing the effect of casino countertactics involve the option of choosing his game. It is transparently clear that whenever a casino's countertactics become too onerous to permit satisfactory play, the player should go elsewhere.

However, many more subtle measures than merely walking away are available to the player to help him reduce the compromising effects that casino countertactics can have. Some have already been discussed in more or less detail, but a unified presentation is now in order.

In order to avoid errors, the player should be sober, reasonably well rested, and prepared to concentrate exclusively on the game. Single-deck games should be preferred to the multiple-deck variety. A bit of exploring will disclose which casinos have the more favorable rules and customs.

It is generally best to play near the third-base position and at an uncrowded table. Card counting is easier when not many players are present. More important, favorable situations will tend to last longer when few people are present to take cards and deplete the deck. If you care to play for amounts larger than the usual minimum bets, many casinos will have one or several tables with a $5 minimum, sometimes one with a $25 minimum, and a rare one with a $100 minimum. For obvious reasons, these tables tend to attract fewer players than the others, and thus they can be chosen to avoid the crowds.

Too much conspicuous table-hopping within a casino is inadvisable. Nevertheless, you often can find it convenient to move from a crowded table to an uncrowded one. Perhaps you have had a run of losses; a change of tables may appear merely to be a superstitious move to get away from a dealer who is "hot." A noisy, unpleasant, or otherwise distracting fellow-player may appear to be your inducement to move. (And sometimes this can be a legitimate as well as a tactical reason. I dislike being at a table with a bad player: the type who doesn't understand the mechanics of the game and who must repeatedly be instructed by the dealer in how to ask for cards, the proper way to indicate a decision to stand, the courtesy of turning up broken hands, and similar matters. Such a player disrupts the rhythm of the game, slows it down, and often déprives the counter of an opportunity to see cards. A drunken player can create the same problems.)

Except as just noted, when the entire casino is crowded, little is usually gained by moving to an uncrowded table; it will soon be crowded too. However, success does not demand an uncrowded table, and often there are some comfortable tactical compensations to be gained by having several other players present. For one thing, casino countertactics are sometimes less readily or less severely invoked with a full complement of players present. Also, with six or seven players, the dealer's shuffling habits usually become quickly predictable. As discussed previously, he often will deal only two rounds of hands before he shuffles. Thus, you can establish a simple, advantageous routine of a small or medium bet on the first hand followed by a minimum or large bet on the second, depending on the point count after the first. Of course, those dealers who sometimes deal a third round before shuffling make the situation even more desirable, and the reverse point count often can be used.

If you are making relatively modest bets, the presence of "high rollers" at the table, playing for amounts in or near the three-figure range, can be a distinct advantage. Even though you are playing a devastating case-down game, an extravagant fellow-player will draw most of the attention.

If a friend is with you and both of you plan to play, you probably will want to choose separate tables. Why should you crowd one another when relatively uncrowded tables provide the best rewards? But if the entire casino is very busy, you will probably be unable to play at uncrowded tables in any event. Thus, you may as well sit together and make sure you see each other's hole cards. Obviously, place five will not be available to both of you, but you can take places four and five. If your friend does not case the deck, he should have no objection to sitting to your right, thus giving you the benefit of seeing all his cards before your turn to draw.

When you have decided to leave the table—to rest a while, change tables, change casinos, etc.—do so at an opportune time. Clearly, you would not want to leave when more hands were about to be dealt from a favorable deck. The player's equivalent of shuffle-up is to quit playing temporarily when the deck has turned unfavorable.

Sometimes, when you are about to take a seat and begin play just after the dealer shuffles, you may be able to delay for a moment to allow him to deal a hand to the other players before you start. Thus, you can take the count and have a running start for that deck at least.

This latter tactic is relatively minor in itself—one to be employed when the opportunity arises but not worth conspicuous seeking. A closely related maneuver, however, can be employed by an expert with casino chips in his pocket, who chooses to stand and watch games, like a curious onlooker, in a crowded casino. He can watch until a deck is highly favorable and the dealer is expected to deal another hand before shuffling. Then the expert can suddenly join the players, without even sitting down, and make a single bet, preferably large. I am not too fond of the technique; if employed enough to offer the player a good chance of any substantial profit, it would become very conspicuous and would take undue time and effort. Nevertheless, it is a stratagem you may want to use now and then when you happen to be present in a casino and, for one reason or another, do not choose to play a sustained session. Still another related stratagem is to play two hands, instead of merely one, at a time when the point count has become favorable.

The preceding section on casino countertactics included a discussion of cheating, which is no real "tactic" at all but merely a form of stealing. The player has no real countertactic against cheating except a suspicious awareness of its possibility. I recommend against *over*suspicion. Depressing runs of bad luck are not uncommon. In practice sessions with my wife or my friends, I have had sustained series of losses that seemed almost incredible in the normal course of events. Yet at those times I knew that the phenomena were merely chance fluctuations, as there was no possibility of anything else. Prolonged variations from "normal" chance expectations are not "abnormal" at all to mathematicians.

Just as you will have streaks of phenomenal wins, you will have others of deplorable losses. These are all mathematically explainable; unfortunately they are unpredictable at a given time, and in the midst of either, there is no way to know when the "luck" will change.

Do not assume you are being cheated every time you lose six or eight hands in a row. Usually you will not be—possibly never. But for your own protection, no great harm will result if you entertain a suspicion. Consider leaving the table if a series of losses is unduly grim, particularly if you have any other reason to think you may be against a cheating dealer. If you leave, the precaution usually will have been unnecessary—you merely were temporarily unlucky. But if the dealer *was* cheating, one thing is certain: your "luck" would never have changed. Since another casino is nearby, you will know at least that you can try again at a similar game without that particular dealer.

Another thing: do not become concerned merely because a dealer draws an "abnormal" number of 21s, 20s, etc. If you play properly, the dealer *must* eventually make many more of these good hands than you, simply because he is required to hit stiffs that you often would not hit. The compensating feature of the rules is that he also will break much more often than you.

Above all, good camouflage, discussed in a previous section, is the most important measure to delay the encountering of casino countertactics. The cornerstone of camouflage is innocuous-appearing bet variation, as discussed in detail in a previous section. However, these betting tactics cannot disguise your expertise indefinitely. I suggest also the advisability of not playing in one casino too long.

Related to this subject is the fact that the casinos usually change shifts about 4:00 A.M., noon, and 8:00 P.M. (These apparently bizarre hours are chosen so that the size of shifts can be tailored to the usual volumes of business during different periods of the day and night.) Ordinarily, new pit bosses arrive a bit ahead of the new dealers to get organized ahead of time. If you are well known to one shift, you may be able to play securely with a later one. But if this is your plan, it is well not to be present during the change of shifts, or the word about you may be passed along. You should also be aware that some dealers, and particularly supervisory personnel, may work split shifts or prolonged shifts. Thus, you cannot totally rely upon the rotation of the clock to reestablish anonymity. Nevertheless, the stratagem is worth remembering.

An important element of camouflage is simply to avoid drawing attention to yourself unnecessarily. Your dress and behavior should be as inconspicuous as possible.

Another possibility for disguising expert ability involves camouflage in the method of *play*. I feel some ambivalence in giving advice about this matter. It requires the disagreeable gambit of sacrificing occasional profitable but sophisticated strategies that might alert the dealer or pit boss to your skill.

Lawrence Revere summarizes this tactic rather simplistically. He advises never to do anything that a bad player would not do. As an example, he states that he would never double down with seven, even though the strategy were mathematically indicated.

A dealer-friend once told me I should avoid drawing to soft 18. Making that draw under correct circumstances, he said, is "a dead giveaway." Another dealer told me I had first given myself away to him by making proper insurance bets. He considers it better to forego most of the insurance profits in an effort to maintain camouflage.

Unlike most dealers, both of my advisers are also expert players. Nevertheless, I cannot generally endorse their advice. I also believe that Revere's generalization was essentially rhetorical—to make a point. If any *one* gambit like those just mentioned, or perhaps two, would guarantee against discovery, then I would certainly play accordingly. But there are too many valuable strategies that deviate from those of the average player to make it practical to sacrifice them all. Most doubling with soft hands, if done correctly, identifies the player as a good one. Further, the variation in drawing to stiff hands against low cards, as the point count fluctuates, must eventually be noticed by an observant, knowledgeable dealer.

Thus, if a dealer is really going to be alerted by your draws to soft 18, or by your insurance strategy, he will eventually catch on anyway. And in the meantime, you will have sacrificed potential winnings.

I do not mean that you should completely disdain camouflage in play. I may forego an unusual, advanced play for camouflage purposes when the indication for the play is borderline. The matter is somewhat comparable to holding a "kicker" to three of a kind in draw poker. There is a small but definitely better chance of improving the hand by drawing two cards. Nevertheless, experts at poker usually draw only one for purposes of deception. At Twenty-One, however, I usually restrict such gambits to borderline decisions. If the point count shows some surprising play to be highly and unequivocally indicated, I go ahead and make it. And naturally, if you know you are already spotted as an expert, you should make no sacrifice in best play. There is no longer any reason for it.

The splitting of 10s deserves special mention regarding camouflage in play. This strategy normally marks a player as an idiot. Thus, if you are unknown and have just begun to play, you may completely disarm the dealer if you are so fortunate as to have a situation rather quickly that calls for the correct splitting of 10s. In such circumstance, it may be well to stretch a point and split a pair if the strategy is *almost* indicated. Probably it will be quite a while before the dealer will realize that you knew what you were doing.

On the other hand, if you have been playing well for a prolonged period, it is difficult to appraise the potential implication of splitting 10s. You may merely confirm what was already suspected: that you are an expert. Or, more favorably, you may achieve the effect previously mentioned and allay suspicion. The difference will depend largely on the expertise of the casino personnel in detecting good play. You must judge for yourself in which way to shade in splitting or not splitting—or whether not to shade at all but to play strictly as the point count dictates.

Finally, a maneuver mentioned in earlier sections can be the most effective of any tactic available to an expert player whenever a casino allows itself to be suitably manipulated. If a dealer begins shuffling each time you make a large bet, simply make moderate bets steadily when the deck is favorable and increase whenever you want a shuffle. On those occasions when you can play prolonged sessions with these conditions, you can win almost every time.

Superstition Behind the Tables

Casino managers and pit bosses are generally as superstitious as other gamblers. One would think that such professionals would understand at least the fundamental principle of the independence of trials, but most do not.

I have seen a pit boss practically go into a frenzy because a particular dealer broke eight times in a row. The slightest understanding of laws of probability would lead anyone to realize that with the many thousands of hands dealt in a large casino every day, *some* dealer must certainly break several times in a row on occasion. But this pit boss ran screaming to his colleagues to have the "unlucky" dealer relieved posthaste. The ignoramus was proudly positive that the dealer who had lost steadily for a few minutes would continue to do so indefinitely. Episodes like this are a way of life in the casinos. Dealers have actually been fired for being unlucky!

I was winning one night when I overheard a shift boss tell the dealer, "Start breaking the deck. He's too good for you."

The *you* in that instruction was illuminating. Unless she was cheating, what difference did it make if that young woman or someone else was dealing the cards? I was, in fact, merely "too good" against the randomly shuffled deck, not against the dealer herself. But the implication was that a "luckier" dealer would have beaten me without "breaking the deck."

The reason for this discussion is to point out the enormous advantage accruing to the expert player from the superstitions of casino personnel. The advantage comes from this: they will seldom worry about you if you are losing.

You may not take too much consolation from being allowed to play a case-down game without great notice if your money is disappearing, but you should. Inevitably, you will have runs of bad luck, just as you will have others of good luck. If the pit bosses were competent, they would understand that too and would be just as concerned about your play at one time as another. Neither they nor you can predict when the luck will change, as it must do, and you will suddenly begin to win. But they are too shortsighted for such discriminations. They are merely greedy and happy when things go against you. Accordingly, during a substantial part of your time at the tables, the casinos' ignorance of the laws of chance will provide the security of unhampered play.

One afternoon at Lake Tahoe, during my first visit to a particular casino, I was in a two-deck game with one other player against a girl dealer. Premature shuffling is relatively uncommon with two decks, but this woman was often shuffling early. I could detect no pattern to her shuffling tendencies; they did not coincide with favorable deck situations or large bets.

After a while the other player left, and the dealer became friendly. She volunteered some advice that I considered nonsensical: "You can't win at this game if you're by yourself."

I was curious about her reasoning, and she explained, "Whenever I break twice in a row, I shuffle." She waited a moment for that news to register and continued, "But if you're the only player, I shuffle every time I *lose* twice in a row, breaking or not."

That seemed to be the custom of the entire casino, dictated by the management. The practice reflected a profound lack of understanding of the fundamentals of 10/X variation. As a case-down player, I would naturally prefer no early shuffling. But if it must occur, the formula of that casino was much to the player's advantage!

True, the dealer will likely lose against good play when the deck is favorable, and win otherwise. But after that normal event has occurred, the cards that brought it about will often have altered the 10/X ratio in a direction to produce a different result with the next hand or two.

If the casino management had been competent, and had wanted to dictate some simplistic formula for shuffling, it would have directed the dealers to shuffle after winning and to continue to deal after losing. Whether its error resulted from an inept effort to reason or from a foolish formula for "stopping a streak" was not evident. In any event, this superstition operates to the player's advantage.

Women

One fascinating superstition that formerly pervaded some casinos was the notion that women brought bad luck. They were unwelcome—and sometimes even barred, if possible. That custom is long past. Modern casinos are frequented by women, and their money is duly cherished.

Still, among the ranks of expert Twenty-One players, the proportion of women is small. The result is a remarkable waste of opportunity. A woman with the odds on her side enjoys a notably greater advantage in a casino than her male counterpart.

First, the sense of chivalry of the male dealers and pit bosses can only operate in her favor. And women dealers are likely to identify more sympathetically with a woman player than with a man.

More important, dealers are not likely to suspect that a demure young beauty or a sedate grandmotherly type can really be an adroit and calculating card counter. Her presumed innocence gives her an inherent element of camouflage that does not accrue to a male gambler.

Shills

The historic role of casino personnel who sit at tables and seem to play as customers is to stimulate business. Popular fantasy often shrouds a person who "plays for the house" with a shadowy aura invoking mistrust. To whatever extent such reputation is deserved, it would apply principally in games where players compete against each other. At Twenty-One, where the players compete entirely against the dealer, the concept of such a person playing "for the house" becomes meaningless in its usual connotation; he can just as well be regarded as playing against the house—but with the house's money.

At Twenty-One, in fact, such a person, known as a *shill*, is not engaged in any contest at all. To avoid any appearance that he is serving as an "anchor man," or that his decisions in playing his hands will have any discretionary influence on the game, he is required to play in a stereotyped, predetermined manner, using "shills' rules." Such rules dictate that the shill never split a pair, never double down, and never draw to a hand that can break. He draws to hard hands that cannot break; he draws or stands with soft hands by mimicking the dealer's formula. Thus, like the dealer, the shill has no options in how to play a hand (although his formula for drawing or standing with hard hands is different). This procedure provides some consolation to superstitious players who often fret that, "He took my card," when a preceding player happens to draw a card that would have helped the other's hand. At least when a shill takes a card that would have helped the next player, no discretion is involved.

Many people are reluctant for some private reason to sit down at a Twenty-One table when no one else is there and thus no game is in progress. Accordingly, a shill frequently will play at an otherwise empty table until regular players join the game.

As previously explained, a few casinos use shills also to prevent an expert from having a head-on game. If a single customer is at a table, a shill promptly joins him. If another customer sits down, the shill leaves. If that other customer then leaves, the shill pops right back from the crowd in the casino and sits down again.

Of course, this practice accommodates those people (obviously nonexperts) who do not like a head-on game. This fact was illustrated by an experience of my wife in one of the downtown Las Vegas casinos. All the players left her table. She was, of course, perfectly pleased with the arrangement, but the dealer did not know that. He asked, "Do you mind playing alone? If you do, I can have a shill come and play until someone sits down."

Casinos generally make no effort to conceal that they use shills—or who the shills are. In fact, some openly reveal the fact by providing these personnel with "shill chips," dummy chips of different color from the others and bearing no monetary denomination.

Mistakes

During an eight-hour shift, with normal relief, a dealer will add a few thousand hands, pay or collect on them, and make change hundreds of times. In theory, the casino demands that he make no mistakes. As a player—a customer—you certainly have the right to expect accuracy.

But honest mistakes inevitably occur, and there is no reason to become incensed when one does happen. They tend to be embarrassing to dealer and player alike. The dealer may pay you the wrong amount. He may add your hand wrong—or his own. Occasionally he may think you want to draw a card before you have decided.

All of these errors are subject to protest. Misinterpretations will generally be resolved in your favor if your argument is reasonable. When an error in the payoff occurs, it is better to point it out before handling the chips.

All hands are picked up in such order that they can be dealt back in case of a question of addition. Occasionally I have been vaguely doubtful about the dealer's accuracy in adding a hand and have not asked for a count-back; I am usually so busy keeping the point count that I do not trust my addition to be superior to the dealer's. But if I am fairly sure a hand has been added wrong, I ask to see it again.

Veteran dealers rarely make mistakes. Novices make them often. Rank beginners have every move closely supervised by one and perhaps more experienced people to prevent any mistakes—in favor of either the player or casino.

Tipping

The custom of tipping prevails in casinos, much as it does in many other businesses providing a service, but under far less rigid standards than in most. It is not mandatory to tip anyone. It is rather fundamental courtesy, however, to tip the cocktail waitress when she serves you.

Whether to tip the dealers is an optional matter, but I usually do so. Inexperienced players often do not tip. For obvious reasons, many players tend to tip more freely when winning than when losing. Some others take the hard-nosed attitude that, "The dealer doesn't tip me when I lose. So why should I tip him when I win?"

I suggest that you follow my custom of tipping the dealer if you play a fairly sustained session and are dealt a reasonably satisfactory game. Whether I win or lose, the vigor and promptness of countertactics and the degree of general courtesy of the casino all have some influence on my generosity. I do not tip a surly and patently hostile dealer. However, I would not withhold at least a nominal tip merely because a dealer has employed a degree of countertactics on the obvious instructions of superiors.

In and around Las Vegas it has been customary, in tipping

a dealer, to drop the chip into his shirt pocket instead of merely handing it to him. Casinos are sensitive about dealers reaching into their pockets or putting anything there themselves. For reasons of anatomy and decorum, however, the recent advent of girl dealers in the Las Vegas area is rendering that custom quaint. Just hand her the tip.

When I tip, instead of simply giving the dealer a chip directly, I often make a bet for him on a hand—in addition to making my own larger bet. I choose a time when the deck is favorable, thus increasing the chance of winning and of doubling the tip. (For camouflage purposes, however, it may be better sometimes to make the tipping bet when the deck is unfavorable.) Of course, if I lose the hand and my bet, the dealer also loses the potential tip to the casino, but he nevertheless appreciates the effort.

In betting a potential tip for the dealer, the sum should be placed separately in front of your own bet. Then, if the hand wins, the two bets are paid separately, and you should hand the dealer his chips or drop them into his shirt pocket.

Even if you are playing only $5 or $25 chips, you usually will soon have some smaller chips in your stack that you may want to use for tipping. These result from the odd-figure payoffs for blackjack and from change received on losing insurance bets. Also, of course, the dealer will give you change if you want it.

A question naturally occurs about whether the custom creates any conflict of interest for the dealers who are, in a sense at least, the players' opponents. The matter is almost not worth consideration. Surveillance is such that a dealer would do nothing improper to help a player win, even in the unlikely event that some mild temptation were felt. Nevertheless, a friendly attitude by a dealer instead of a hostile one can clearly do no harm. At least he may be less inclined to shuffle prematurely, hide cards, and so forth, unless a pit boss firmly requires him to do so. If such matters are of any concern to the casinos, the control is entirely in their hands. If they chose, they could increase the dealers' salaries and forbid the acceptance of tips.

All dealers' tips are pooled and shared equally by those on the shift. Tips account for a substantial portion of the dealers' incomes.

Pit bosses do not accept tips.

Rules Variations

There are several variations in rules between different casinos. To appraise the prospects at any given game, it is helpful to have some general idea of the effect of each variation.

It is obvious, of course, that restrictions on the players' options diminish the expert's profits. Fortunately for us, though, every "liberal" rule but one (dealers' standing on all 17s) adds to the casinos' rate of winning from the far more numerous ordinary players. The more opportunities these people have to follow unsound strategies, the more they tend to lose. Thus, the casinos face a dilemma when they must choose between restrictive and freer rules: to penalize us they must sacrifice an element of their advantage over their unskilled opponents.

I must emphasize that the exact quantitative effect of each rule on our potential advantage defies precise calculation. Quite close calculations have been made for their influence when *basic* strategy is used. For example, Thorp presents a list of such data, based partly upon calculations of the Baldwin group. However, in our point-count method, the variations in size of bets and strategy of play lead to significant deviations from these norms. Also, the difference in frequency of shuffling between casinos and individual dealers contributes to the degree of deviation in any particular game.

The variation in the effect of the soft-17 rule provides an illustration. Thorp states that when the dealer draws to soft 17s instead of standing, the house gains an advantage of 1/5 of 1% (0.002). With the Archer point-count system, however, the effect of the rule is probably less serious. The reason is that the rule works its greatest disadvantage to the player at negative point counts, when bets are small; at high positive counts, when bets are large, the effect of the rule is minimal. True, whatever effect the rule does have at high point counts is more costly then, which complicates analysis of the problem. After balancing all factors, however, I am persuaded that the soft-17 rule reduces the advantage of the card counter somewhat less than the theoretical 1/5 percent.

On the other hand, the inability to double down with less than 10 or 11 is somewhat more disadvantageous to an expert than the theoretical figure would suggest. This rule works about a 1/4 percent disadvantage in basic strategy. However, the expanding indications for doubling in the situations with high point counts and high bets clearly show that our advantage is reduced by more than 1/4 percent. I would estimate that the advantage is reduced by about 1/3 percent when we are deprived of these opportunities.

From all this comes an explanation of a generalization I made earlier about the difference between your advantage in a typical Las Vegas casino and that in a typical northern Nevada casino. I estimated a 2 percent advantage at the Las Vegas game. That figure was based upon both the empirical results of my own record in play and extrapolations from the convergent trend of computer calculations, each method confirming the other. The figure is perhaps a bit conservative, but it allows for the occasional mistakes in play and for the approximations to ideal play incorporated into my system. The difference in how casinos in the Las Vegas area draw to 17 has only a trivial influence on the estimate. (Strip casinos stand with soft 17; those downtown draw.) However, the *combined* effect of the soft-17 rule and the restrictions on doubling probably reduce your advantage in most Reno-Tahoe casinos to little if any more than 1½ percent.

Failure to offer insurance is another variation found in some Reno casinos—usually the smaller ones. I have calculated the approximate value of insurance betting in my system and estimate that it accounts for more than 1/8 and probably closer to 1/7 of the profit (assuming the 2 percent advantage). It accounts for more than 1/6 of the profit in Reno. To state the matter differently, the insurance opportunities alone provide an advantage between 1/4 percent and 1/3 percent greater than the even odds of basic strategy. In a Reno casino that restricts doubling to 10 and 11, draws to soft 17, *and* fails to offer insurance, your advantage is probably no more than 1¼ percent. (In fact, if that casino combines its bad rules with aggressive early shuffling, the advantage may not be above 1%.)

Some casinos permit doubling down on the hands obtained after a pair is split. This option probably adds about 1/5 percent to the advantage of the expert. The figure is somewhat higher than Thorp's and Wilson's calculations would indicate, but I repeat: previous appraisals analyzed the effect of rules in basic strategy. For the point-count player, the option to double after splitting assumes added value.

The surrender rule, so conducive to mistakes by poor players, provides substantial savings of potentially losing bets for the expert. Epstein has given the overall advantage of the rule in basic strategy as about 1/7 percent (0.0015). He assumed a different type of surrender rule from the one played in Nevada. Nevertheless, offsetting features in when the player may opt under the classic rule as compared to the Nevada rule would tend to validate the figure for the basic strategy player in Nevada also. But for the expert, the surrender option is clearly more valuable than for the basic player. The expert will decline surrender at low point counts and, more importantly, will choose it in increasingly more situations at high counts when bets are large. I am confident that the surrender rule must add nearly 1/4 percent to the card counter's advantage when employed properly.

A note should be added about resplitting of pairs (you split a pair of 8s, receive another 8, and split that new pair too). The option to resplit Aces is now obsolete. However, a few Las Vegas casinos also forbid resplitting of other pairs. This restriction is disagreeable but not of major importance. In basic strategy, only trival gains are provided overall by resplitting of new pairs. A principal interest of the rule to an expert is the inability to resplit 10s. While that compromising feature (among the others) can occasionally deprive you of some profits, the occurrence is uncommon. In short, the value of the standard rule, by which pairs *can* be resplit, cannot account for as much as 1/10 of 1 percent of your advantage.

One more rule should be mentioned in passing, even though it is obsolete in Nevada. In the past many casinos permitted doubling down after drawing any number of cards. Say you started with 4,3 and drew another 4, for a total of 11. As you know, you usually would double down with that total. To the expert, this rule should be worth about 1/4 percent advantage.

(I might mention that Twenty-One is still played occasionally at private clubs and parties in which the dealer wins all ties. No player can expect to win at such a game. Even with best* play, the percentage disadvantage is worse than at roulette.)

The common rules variations are summarized in the following outline. They are listed in order of their estimated importance. I do not include their values in fractions of a percent, as that might imply a precision greater than my informed estimates would warrant. Simply remember that number 1 is far more important (1/3 percent player's advantage) than number 6 (< 1/10 percent). Appraise the relative value of the others in accord with the preceding discussion.

1. Doubling allowed on any first two cards (not just on 10 and 11).
2. Insurance offered.
3. Surrender allowed.
4. Doubling allowed after pair-splitting.
5. Dealer stands on all 17s (no "soft-17 rule").
6. Resplitting of pairs allowed.

If you have any difficulty in appraising the fractions I have used in this section, just recall the implications of a 2 percent advantage on your expected yield. If you play 100 hands and your average bet is $10, you should win about $20. A 1/5 percent change in advantage, because of some rule variation, would reduce the expectation to $18 or raise it to $22, depending upon the direction of the change. If, through the cumulative effect of rules variations, your advantage is only 1.5 percent, you could expect only $15 under the other stated conditions; if it is 2.5 percent, you could expect $25.

---

*I should point out that against a dealer who wins ties, best play would require many changes from the strategy of this book. You would stand more often and double down much less often.

It is important to remember, however, that good or bad customs by a casino can be more significant than one or two rules. Differences in tendencies to shuffle late or early, to hide cards or not, and similar matters vary greatly between casinos. These factors can have a substantial influence on your advantage. The estimated figures I have given relate to average conditions.

I should emphasize that my geographical references in this section relate only to *trends* in the casinos. You can find an occasional casino in northern Nevada with better rules than some others in the Las Vegas area.

Before leaving this subject, I should alert you to a rather peculiar instability that pervades the casino business. You can never be sure that things will be the same from one day to the next. A casino in Reno may adopt very liberal rules and customs for a while and then alter one or both conditions. Another may simultaneously vacillate in the other direction. The Strip is a bit less erratic, but there too a casino may adopt a new rule or variation in customs and soon change again.

More than once I have been amused to see a dealer forget the rules of the casino in which he was working. A few years ago, for example, all the downtown casinos in Las Vegas agreed to forbid resplitting after an initial pair had been split. Repeatedly, I saw dealers invoke the rule at one moment and then fail to do so a short time later. In any event, the habitual players did not like the restriction. Before long, at least five of these casinos had abandoned it.

11

Multiple-Deck Games

LARGELY in an effort to counteract the effectiveness of expert players, many casinos have introduced a game in which four decks are shuffled together and dealt from a specially constructed box, called a "shoe." These devices are almost standard paraphernalia in Europe and in the Caribbean. In the Las Vegas area a few casinos now provide only this type of game. Some others offer a variety—some single-deck and some four-deck games. A few also have some two-deck games; these are not dealt from a shoe; instead they resemble the single-deck game except that two decks are shuffled together. Multiple-deck games are rare in northern Nevada, but occasionally they are seen.

While most card-counting players prefer the single-deck game, and for good reason, I think a real mastery of Twenty-One requires the ability to cope with multiple decks as well. For one thing, you may want to play where nothing else is offered.

Four-deck games are less desirable to an expert than are single-deck games. Fortunately, ordinary players tend to dislike four decks also, and thus the single decks remain in vogue through popular demand. It is interesting to observe the maneuvering of the management of some casinos in offering the two types. During busiest times, when the casino is very crowded, most or even all games may be with four decks; the management knows it will have a good business at the tables regardless of what it offers. But during slack periods, when the "buyers' market" exists, the single-deck offerings will predominate.

The most fundamental reason for avoiding the four-deck game is the existence of an inherent small but definite statistical disadvantage against all players, novice and expert alike, that does not exist with the single deck game. Recall that with a single deck, the basic-strategy player is essentially on even terms with the casino (slightly more or less, depending on rules in force) when the deck has been freshly shuffled and the deal commences. But not so with four decks. A fraction of a percent disadvantage exists.*

Actually, if ideal rules were in force, basic strategy *would* put the player on equal terms with the four-deck game or even ahead of it. But they never are. And with rather typical rules, the player begins against a fundamental house advantage

---

*Since the ratio of cards in a full four decks is the same as in a full single deck, it may seem incongruous that the basic odds are different. The reason is the difference in effect of partial depletion. A simplified analogy may help explain. Imagine a "deck" of only three cards: a 10, an Ace, and an X. Now, suppose you hold the 10 and will receive one of the other two cards chosen at random. Your chance of getting the Ace for a blackjack is obviously one in two. However, imagine another deck of *two* 10s, two Aces, and two Xs. Initially, the ratios of these cards are the same as in the preceding deck of three cards. But now give yourself one of the 10s. When you then draw one of the other five cards at random, your chances of drawing an Ace for a blackjack are only two in five, a less favorable prospect than in the preceding example.

between one-third and one-half of a percent. Thus the expert's potential winnings from increasing his bets in favorable situations do not represent all clear profit; these winnings must first overcome the moderate losses to be expected while playing with the deck near neutral.

In addition, the diluting effect of 208 cards as opposed to 52 reduces the frequency of favorable situations. Since the last several cards are generally not dealt, *highly* favorable situations are quite rare.

Further, the four-deck game moderately increases the difficulty of card counting. Numbers, both positive and negative, tend to run higher, and this probably leads to a few more errors. Also, because of the long time between shuffles, the effect of errors in counting is more sustained.

A compensating feature of four decks largely ameliorates the latter problem. If a counting error occurs, it is only one-fourth as serious in the play of any individual hand as with a single deck. The four-deck game provides a few other compensating advantages. They are inadequate to overcome the disadvantages, but they are important nevertheless.

For one thing, when favorable situations occur, they tend to last longer than in the conventional, single-deck game. This is partly for the same reason that reduces their frequency of occurrence in the first place: the diluting effect of the many cards tends to stabilize the 10/X (10s to non-10s) ratio wherever it may be.

Particularly important, the nature of the four-deck game makes the casino countertactic of premature shuffling impractical. Although the last few cards are not dealt, the decks are routinely dealt near to the end.

Finally, extremely unfavorable deck compositions are less common with the four-deck game. This, of course, does not compensate for the corresponding relative rareness of favorable situations, as bets are small in the former circumstance and large in the latter. But it does lessen the inherent disadvantage of the game to some degree.

I have not played the four-deck game extensively (why should I?), but I have had some experience with it and have experimented enough in practice, keeping careful records, to know that it can be beaten.

A somewhat larger amount of initial capital is needed in relation to the minimum bet than for the single-deck game. Certain adjustments are required in the method previously presented for the conventional game.

The point-count method presented previously for deriving the 10/X ratio adapts nicely to the multiple-deck game. It is kept just as before, counting plus 1 for each X and minus 2 for each 10. The count begins at zero, before any cards are seen from the freshly shuffled decks.

However, the significance of a given point-count total with four decks is only one-fourth that with the conventional game. Thus, a count of plus 16 is ordinarily needed before the deck can be considered sufficiently favorable to increase the size of bets. At plus 16, the strategy changes should be made for playing hands that otherwise were made at plus 4.* Bear in mind also that when about one-fourth of the cards (52) are dealt, plus 4 will represent a neutral deck; when half (104) are dealt, plus 8 will represent it; and when three-fourths (156) are dealt, plus 12 will represent it. Similarly, for the excellent deck ordinarily represented by about plus 8, a count of plus 32 will be needed with one-fourth of the cards gone (a highly unlikely occurrence), plus 28 will be needed with half gone (not *too* uncommon), and plus 24 will be needed with three-fourths gone. And so forth. The point-count values

---

*One exception will be mentioned presently.

given in previous chapters must be multiplied by four to derive the approximate same significance in playing the four-deck game.

A reasonably good strategy for the four-deck game can be devised simply by making these four-fold extrapolations. Do so if you wish to avoid the tedium of learning the next few pages. The relatively wide ranges between strategy changes, however, would deprive us of some precision associated especially with multiple decks. If you plan to play the four-deck game extensively (as in England or the Caribbean, for example), you eventually should learn the refinements of this chapter.

In the following presentation, I shall assume that you firmly understand the concept from previous chapters of the varying significance of the point count when the decks are full and when they are depleted. When few cards remain, a point count near plus 16 will indicate the same 10/X ratio as a count far removed from plus 16 with the decks nearly full. Plus 16 itself, however, always indicates a ratio of 0.5.

Basic Strategy with Four Decks

Basic strategy is used with a neutral deck (ranging between 0 and plus 16 as cards are dealt). However, slightly greater efficiency will be achieved by making a few changes from the basic strategy (Chapter 2) for the single-deck game.

Draw to soft 18 vs. Act (i.e., vs. 9, 10, or Ace).
Do not double down with 11 vs. Ace.
Do not double down with 9 vs. 2.
Do not double down with soft 18 vs. 3.
Do not double down with soft 13 vs. 4.

The multiple-deck game has produced an anachronism: when Baldwin and his colleagues first published a scientific basic strategy, they recommended drawing to 11 against Ace instead of doubling. We now revert to that tactic (plus a couple of other Baldwin recommendations).

When the point count approaches half way between neutral and plus 16, discontinue the preceding changes and return essentially to the full basic strategy. Make one adjustment: stand with hard 16 against 10 instead of drawing.

Plus 16—A Good Deck

When the point count reaches plus 16 or exceeds that figure, adopt the strategy changes listed in Chapter 4. These are the changes invoked at plus 4 in the single-deck game. I will not list them here again. You should know them already, but can easily review them if you have forgotten anything. One exception should be noted: draw to hard 15 against 10 instead of standing. We will wait for a slightly higher point count, to be discussed presently, before standing in that situation.

In the four-deck game, insurance should be taken with any point count above plus 16. It should never be taken below plus 16.

In the strategy variations that follow, you will notice patterns reminiscent of those in Chapters 7 and 8. However, the 10/X ranges will be narrower between series of adjustments.

For your convenience in memorizing, the point-count values that follow are rounded off, either to even numbers or multiples of 5. Thus they sometimes only approximate the 10/X ratio under consideration. This compromise, however, introduces only trivial error.

Further Adjustments with Favorable Decks

It is vital that point counts be read in correct context. In the first two sets of adjustments, they are identified as being correct at plus 24 and plus 30 respectively. These figures assume that the decks are one-half dealt. A larger or smaller count is correct under other conditions. For example, to illustrate a 10/X ratio of 0.55, I give a point count thus: plus 24 (+ 30 → + $\underline{24}$ → + 20). This means that with only one-fourth of the cards dealt, plus 30 is required; and with three-fourths dealt, plus 20 is enough.

At plus 24 (+ 30 → + $\underline{24}$ → + 20) (10/X $\cong$ 0.55):
Stand with hard 15 vs. 10.
Always double down with 10.
Double down with soft 19 vs. 4.
Double down with soft 14, 15, and 16 vs. 3.
Split 10s vs. 5 or 6.

At plus 30 (+ 40 → + $\underline{30}$ → + 24) (10/X = 0.62):
Stand with hard 16 vs. 9.
Stand with hard 14 vs. 10.
Double down with 9 vs. 8.
Double down with 8 vs. 4.
Double down with soft 20 vs. 5 or 6.
Double down with soft 19 vs. 3.
Double down with soft 15 and 16 vs. 2.
Double down with soft 13 vs. 3.
Split 10s vs. 4.
Split 9s vs. 7.
Do not split 8s vs. 10.

There is little reason to think of the next set of adjustments except in terms of far-depleted decks—with only 50 or 60 uncounted cards remaining. Accordingly, the point-count designation should be regarded in the context that about three-fourths of the four decks have been counted. (Note, as always, that plus 30 very late in the excursion through the decks has a far different significance than when half the cards remain.)

At plus 30 late (. . . → + 45 → + <u>30</u>) ($10/X \cong 0.77$):
Stand with hard 16 vs. Ace.
Stand with hard 15 vs. 9 or Ace.
Stand with hard 13 vs. 10.
Double down with 8 vs. 2 or 3.
Double down with 7 vs. 5 or 6.
Double down with all soft hands vs. 2 through 6.
Split 10s vs. 2 or 3.
Split 9s vs. Ace.
If doubling down with 8 is not permitted, split 4s against 5 or 6.

I could add one more set of adjustments for favorable decks —to be made at plus 40 late in the deal. However, the 10/X ratio that this represents is too rare with four decks to justify cluttering your brain. (In fact, the count in the neighborhood of 40 that I have placed in preceding parentheses is essentially academic in actual play.)

You may have noticed that a pair of 7s has no unusual significance in the multiple-deck game. It is split only against 2 through 7 and otherwise handled like any other hard 14.

With that exception, surrender is played essentially as in the single-deck game. With the decks about neutral, surrender with hard 15 or 16 against 10. At higher point counts, surrender (if it is allowed) with stiff hands when the strategy otherwise calls for standing against a high card. Any close decision of this type is best resolved in favor of surrender.

Adjustments with Unfavorable Decks

In considering point counts with unfavorable decks, we will begin again, for the first three sets of adjustments, with the assumption that the decks are dealt about half through. The counts in parentheses show ranges representing degrees of depletion from one-fourth to three-fourths.

While we know that zero is the neutral count with the decks freshly shuffled, zero represents a 10/X ratio of 0.4 with half the cards dealt. That is the condition assumed for the first adjustments.

Remember from the early pages of this chapter the revisions in the basic strategy that are made with four-deck games. These revisions will continue to be played at any unfavorable point count. Additional changes are made as the decks become progressively unfavorable.

At zero (-8 → 0 → + 8) (10/X ≅ 0.4):
   Always draw to hard 12.
   Draw to hard 13 vs. 2 or 3.
   Do not double down with 10 vs. 9.
   Do not double down with 9 vs. 3.
   Double down with soft 17 (or 18) only vs. 4, 5, or 6.
   Double down with soft 13 through 16 only vs. 5 or 6.
   Do not split Aces vs. Ace.
   Do not split 2s, 3s, 6s, or 9s vs. 2.
   Split 3s vs. 8.
   Do not surrender.

At minus 8 (-20 → -8 → +4) (10/X ≅ 0.33):
   Always draw to hard 13.
   Draw to hard 14 vs. 2 or 3.
   Double down with 10 and 11 only vs. 2 through 7.
   Double down with 9 only vs. 5 or 6.
   Do not double down with soft 13, 14, or 15.
   Do not split 6s or 9s vs. 3.

At minus 16 (-35 →-16 → +2) (10/X < 0.3):
   Always draw to hard 14.
   Draw to hard 15 vs. 2 or 3.
   Draw to hard 17 vs. Ace.
   Do not double down with 9.
   Double down with soft 18 only vs. 5.
   Double down with soft 17 only vs. 5 or 6.
   Double down with soft 16 only vs. 6.
   Split Aces only vs. 2 through 7.
   Split 9s only vs. 5 or 9.
   Split 6s only vs. 5 or 6.

The next adjustment can be ignored except very late through the decks (only about one-fourth uncounted). Notice the extreme difference between the significance of zero at that time in comparison with half the decks remaining.

At zero late (. . . → -30 → _0_) (10/X ≅ 0.22):
   Always draw to hard 15.
   Draw to hard 16 vs. 2 or 3.
   Double down with 10 and 11 only vs. 4, 5, or 6.
   Do not double down with soft 16 or 18.
   Split Aces only vs. 5 or 6.
   Do not split 6s or 9s at all.
   Split 3s vs. 9.
   Split 2s vs. 8.
   Do not split 2s vs. 3.

As with the previous consideration of favorable decks, one more adjustment with unfavorable decks could be given. But the circumstance of a 10/X ratio of less than 0.2 is just too rare with four decks to make the matter worthwhile. If you *should* encounter a point count around minus 6 with three-fourths of the decks counted, simply draw to all stiffs and do not double down with anything. The other adjustments that theoretically should be made occur too rarely to be mentioned.

The changes in pair-splitting strategy with unfavorable point counts are tedious. If you prefer merely to approximate with little loss of efficiency, just use basic strategy except for one set of adjustments.

> *At approximately minus 12 (-25 → -12 → +4), roughly half way through the decks:*
> Split Aces only vs. 2 through 7.
> Do not split 6s or 9s at all.

I recognize the contradictions contained in this adjustment, but it represents a broad generalization. I prefer greater precision than that simplistic adjustment provides. Against the four-deck game, you should fight for every possible advantage.

General Measures to Beat the Four-Deck Game

A clear necessity in playing the four-deck game is to make *much* larger bet increases when the deck is favorable than were recommended with the camouflaging betting schemes recommended for the conventional game. Remember: favorable situations occur less frequently, and it also is necessary to win enough when they do occur to overcome the small losses that probably will occur when the deck is neutral. Camouflage in betting must be largely abandoned, but fortunately, the casino is essentially deprived of its prime countertactic, the early shuffle.

I suggest absolute minimum or near-minimum bets in this game until a count of plus 16 is reached (shade this downward

no more than a point or two *early* during the excursion
through the decks, and none at all late). At plus 16 or higher,
bet five, ten, or twenty units—the higher the count, the larger
your bet. Obviously, to avoid gambler's ruin, you will need
a substantially large amount of capital in relation to the size
of your minimum bet. Without it, a run of bad luck can easily
wipe you out in this four-deck game if you play a betting
strategy that gives a good prospect of success.

The separate count of Aces is not so valuable in this game
as otherwise. Their number (16) adds to the difficulty of
keeping track of it, and highly significant variations from
normal are not to be expected very often. Some advantage may
accrue, however, from keeping a general estimate of the Ace
count and merely "leaning" in one direction or another in the
size of bets if an unusual disproportion occurs at a point count
on the borderline of favorability.

Please recall that in some of these games, all cards except
the dealer's hole card are dealt face up. This practice does not
facilitate card counting as much as you might think. The
pace of the game is less even. When a player's hand is such
that a decision to stand is virtually obvious, the dealer tends
almost to make it for the player and passes him by quickly.
Broken hands are gathered in very rapidly.

With this technique of dealing I find card counting to be
much simpler once I have the problem of playing my own
hand over with. I am confident that your experience will be
the same. Accordingly, I recommend a place near first base
instead of third, preferably place two at a six-place table or
place three at a seven-place table.

Other Multiple-Deck Games

Some casinos in Europe employ a six-deck game with a
shoe. This merely introduces an exaggeration of various
effects discussed with four decks. Plus 24 represents the favor-

able 0.5 10/X ratio. That count, of course, occurs less readily than the plus 16 with four decks. At least, however, the extra cards provide more time to reach it. If the six-deck game is played, increase all point count requirements by 50 percent over those presented for strategy adjustments with four decks.

The six-deck game is not offered in Nevada. A two-deck game, however, is played in a few casinos. This game is intermediate in fundamental disadvantage between the conventional and the four-deck games. Usually, all cards are dealt face up. Premature shuffling is not too common. Thus, the game, while not preferred, is at least acceptable to an expert.

Again, bets must be quite large when the deck is favorable (plus 8 or higher with two decks) and minimal otherwise. Insurance is taken at plus 9 or higher. If you understand the adjustments in the significance of the point count for the four-deck game, you will have no difficulty in making comparable adjustments for the two-deck game: point count totals have just half the significance of those discussed in the detailed presentations in other chapters for the single deck; thus, double each point count total, plus or minus, to adapt to the two-deck game. And remember the "sliding" values toward plus 8.

I recommend that with two decks you modify the basic strategy as outlined for the four-deck game. About midway between a neutral deck and plus 8, return to the full basic strategy (Chapter 2) but stand with hard 16 against 10 at this point.

For other strategy adjustments, I recommend that you adapt the system given in Chapters 4, 7, and 8, instead of extrapolating from the four-deck strategy of this chapter.

12

Losers Are Our Friends

As I was winning one night in Reno, I noticed casually the idiotic play of a high-rolling loser. The pit boss, who evidently knew the player, was jovial. He asked the man, "Why don't you just mail your money in to us? That would save you the trouble of coming out here."

I presume that the player could afford his losses. I always hope that any bad player can do so. But however that may be, one thing is certain: the superstitious, guessing, misinformed, inept players are essential for our purpose. They provide the enormous profits to the casinos that keep the game of Twenty-One alive. They are our benefactors; we take a little of their losses back from the tables. I do hope they enjoy themselves. That is about the only return available to most casino gamblers.

And the bulk of the casinos' income is not from the high-rollers who make three-figure bets. It is the far more numerous small players, whose bets are confined to the one-figure range, who provide the greatest profits. These dollar players are known in the casino business as the "grinds," because of the process of grinding out their money, bit by bit. Frankly, I should think that a more complimentary title could be invented for them; without them the Nevada casinos would wither away.

Can the Game Survive?

Shortly after the first edition of Edward Thorp's *Beat the Dealer* received publicity, a mild panic seized the casino managers. They feared a sudden swarm of newly-made experts at the Twenty-One tables and an end to profits from the game. Consequently, the casinos on the Las Vegas Strip simultaneously introduced drastic restrictions on doubling down and splitting pairs. All that resulted was a precipitous drop in regular business. (And according to Thorp and Wilson, the experts continued to play anyway—and to win, although naturally at a reduced rate.)

The rules changes did not last long. When the casinos realized that they were driving away their regular customers, who habitually lost but who had come to enjoy a certain type of game and would not tolerate the restricted one, the old rules reappeared about as fast as they had vanished shortly before. Since then, there has been far from any avalanche of skilled case-down players to overwhelm the casinos. I think I have noticed a gradual, moderate improvement in basic play, but not enough to reduce the casinos' percentage to any great degree. Most players continue in their uninformed and inevitably losing ways. Certainly, the number of experts has increased, but they still represent only a minute fraction of the players of the game. To counteract the mild trend toward better average play, the casinos have gradually introduced rather minor and subtle rules changes (see Chapter 10), increased the tendency to shuffle up, and instituted the four-deck games.

The question is, will a steady encroachment on the rules and conditions of the traditional game eventually eliminate it? Certainly, the casinos could not continue to offer a game if it ever came to cost them money—or merely failed to provide a satisfactory profit. And the number of experts clearly is going to increase; if this book serves its purpose, it, of itself, will increase the number. But for some time now, at least eight books that present winning methods in detail have been available. More than three others have given the basic strategy with only the most minor variations. In view of all this, it seems that if the present game were going to become unprofitable for the casinos, the event already would have occurred, or at least that good signs would be in view that the time is approaching. Yet nothing of the sort appears to be true.

Naturally, I cannot positively predict that the four-deck games and restrictive rules will never completely replace the traditional game. But the casinos must compete with each other for customers, and I have repeatedly observed public preference to influence the casinos' offerings. Empty tables where the four-deck shoes are present prompt a gratifying reappearance of the single-deck game. Probably the greatest danger is if the general public ever comes complacently to accept the four decks and the shoe. It is discomfiting to see an occasional player actually seek out a shoe game with the notion that he *prefers* it! (I suppose such people think the shoe device protects them against cheating. It is interesting that the last two cheating scandals in the Las Vegas area involved games dealt from a shoe.) Fortunately, the great majority of ordinary players who have any preference at all seem to dislike the shoe almost as much as the experts do. This fact tends to give hope for the future—unless *too* many people learn to win and thus force the casinos to alter the game further.

If you have studied and mastered this book, and if you bear in mind that several fine books on the game have long been readily available, you may come to wonder why so few expert players are to be seen in the casinos. The explanation, I think, lies in human habits. The "simple" game of Twenty-One is difficult to learn to play well. Each of several authors, in his own way, has presented a winning method of play. (Perhaps I should say *the* winning method, because masters of any of the sound books would play the great majority of hands in the same way, given similar deck compositions, and no one would be seriously in error when there were differences.) My own technique has been didactic. I have presented fairly detailed explanations of progressive changes in playing strategy, often with approximations to aid simplicity, in conjunction with an easy and practical system of casing the deck. Yet, despite all my efforts to make your task easier, if you have really *learned* the material, you have had to *work*. You have had to study and to practice in simulated play.

Most people are not willing to apply this effort. In my judgment the reason the panic in the casinos was unwarranted, after Dr. Thorp published *Beat the Dealer*, was that most people who read the book discovered that it did not magically open their heads and pour in knowledge. The book was a magnificent revelation: to the usual run of casino gambler, it should have been somewhat equivalent to the discovery of fire or the invention of the wheel. But learning even the simplest of the systems he presented took a bit of effort—and that apparently was too much. Continuing to lose at the tables, by whatever technique, was easier: hitting all stiffs, standing on all stiffs, failing to double down, splitting pairs without insight, taking insurance by superstitious criteria, or whatever.

It is more difficult to understand why the overwhelming majority of players remain ignorant of *basic* strategy. It is relatively easy to learn, and it has been frequently published. But learning even basic strategy requires *some* effort. And I know many habitual poker players with fair native intelligence who cannot bring themselves to apply any energy to reading and understanding such books as those by Morehead,[17] Jacoby,[18] Scarne,[15] or Rubens.[19] Similarly, many people play bridge for years and never do more than read and largely forget some summary of a bidding system, garner through hearsay some fragmentary information and misinformation on playing strategy, and continue to pick up hands, bid, and play the cards in a fog of naivete. They vaguely realize that bids should convey some message to their partners, that there may be some kind of signal besides the high-low, and that advanced technique of declarers' play may involve something more than the simple finesse. But they never bring themselves to read, and *study*, a complete book by Goren[20] or any other expert to gain a reasonable understanding of the game they are trying to play.

In short, many people, whether engaged in bridge, poker, Twenty-One, or numerous other enterprises not related to card games, seem to insulate themselves against improvement. Often they are so bad that they cannot realize, or at least will not admit to themselves, that the possibility of improvement exists. Also, to the novice, much advice from experts appears strange, is not promptly understood, and thus may be rejected. Good play of Twenty-One requires measures that astonish many people who do not have insight into the fine points. Failing to understand the reasoning and mathematics behind proper play, they choose to substitute their own judgment for that of the experts and continue to squander their money through bad play.

Another reason for continued bad play is a substantial body of literature that provides strategies seriously at variance with those that are mathematically sound. Faced with conflicting advice in print, many readers are unable to discriminate between what is sound and what is unsound. Also, many others may never happen to encounter any but one or more of the inferior published strategies.

For all these reasons, I believe that Blackjack will likely survive in essentially its present form. If it does not, we can take consolation that we can *still* win against the multiple-deck game and the shoe.

In discussing the future of the game, I should mention that prospects appear fairly bright for the legalization of casinos in states other than Nevada. At this writing, political stirrings suggest that New Jersey may be first. But however that may be, it is predictable that some states in the East, and probably elsewhere, will eventually have legally sanctioned casinos.

Gambling in some form is already legal in most states. (No state, including Nevada, legalizes *all* forms.) From the player's standpoint, most casino games are far more generous in house odds than most legal gambling elsewhere.

In comparison with most other state-sanctioned gambling, the average casino game takes only a relatively modest percent of the action. And against a Twenty-One game with any kind of reasonable rules, even a bad player has a far better chance than the average visitor to a race track.

End It

Early in this book, I suggested that a fully satisfactory motive for playing Twenty-One is enjoyment of the game. If you make a profit, that is all the better. Please recognize that sometimes you must lose; your percentage advantage is not enough to forestall occasional bouts of bad fortune. But with good play, you should win more often than you lose.

But I think there are more rewards from a successful endeavor than the purely tangible. Most experts at whatever pursuit take satisfaction in their accomplishments, important or otherwise. Why else would bridge players travel across states, continents, and oceans merely to compete with their colleagues for master points, redeemable in nothing but recognition by their peers? Why else would young athletes, particularly those without professional ambition, struggle long and tiringly to try to win for their schools? Many people strive at many tasks purely for the pride of excellence.

There is little explicit recognition accorded the expert at Twenty-One except the stacks of chips he often will carry to the cashier's window. But now and then, in the midst of furious play, an unexpected comment may come from the dealer: "You play an excellent game, Sir. I don't see many experts here. It's an honor to deal to you." That is a verbatim statement a dealer made to me one night in downtown Las Vegas. I remember that I was very tired at the time and not even playing my best game. Unsolicited compliments like that, when offered in obvious sincerity as this one was, are rare. They are not given when other people can hear—particularly the pit bosses. But I have received a few others like that one. I suppose the gratification is a matter of pure vanity, but a recognition from peers is greatly satisfying.

The ubiquitous salutation in Nevada is "Good Luck." One of my bridge partners recently told me that a superstition exists that it is "bad luck" to wish "Good Luck" to a gambler. Well, the vagaries of chance certainly affect winning and losing, and fortune is predictable only in statistical terms, but superstition does not affect the 10/X ratio. As Twenty-One involves gambling, good or bad luck will influence the outcome, but there is no way to conjure either. Expert play involves much more methodical application of mathematics and logic than luck. Nevertheless, I indulge myself the privilege of wishing my readers: Good Luck.

Notes

1. Baldwin, R.R., Cantey, W.E., Maisel, H., and McDermott, J.P. "The Optimum Strategy in Blackjack," *Journal of the American Statistical Association,* 51:429-439 (Sept.), 1956.

2. ——— *Playing Blackjack to Win: A New Strategy for the Game of 21,* New York: M. Barrows, 1957.

3. Thorp, E.O. "Fortune's Formula: The Game of Blackjack," *Notices of the American Mathematical Society,* 935-936 (Dec.), 1960.

4. ——— "A Favorable Strategy for Twenty-One," *Proceedings of the National Academy of Sciences.* 47:110-112, 1961.

5. ——— *Beat the Dealer.* New York: Random House, 1962.

6. ——— *Beat the Dealer,* new ed. New York: Vintage Books, 1966.

7. Wilson, A.N. *The Casino Gambler's Guide.* New York: Harper & Row, 1965

8. Epstein, R.A. *The Theory of Gambling and Statistical Logic.* New York: Academic Press, 1967.

9. Revere, L. *Playing Blackjack As a Business.* Las Vegas: Paul Mann, 1971.

10. Einstein, C. *How to Win at Blackjack.* New York: Cornerstone Library, 1968.

11. Scharff, R. *The Las Vegas Expert's Gambling Guide.* New York: Grosset & Dunlap, 1968.

12. Jacoby, O. *Oswald Jacoby on Gambling.* Garden City, N.Y.: Doubleday, 1963.

13. Collver, D.L. *Scientific Blackjack and Complete Casino Guide.* New York: Arco, 1966.

14. Levinson, H.C. *The Science of Chance.* London: Faber and Faber, 1952.

15. Scarne, J. *Scarne on Cards.* New York: Crown, 1949.

16. McQuaid, C. *Gambler's Digest.* Northfield, Ill.: Digest Books, 1971.

17. Morehead, A. *The Complete Guide to Winning Poker.* New York: Simon and Schuster, 1967.

18. Jacoby, O. *Oswald Jacoby on Poker,* revised ed. Garden City, N.Y.: Doubleday, 1947.

19. Rubens, J. *Win at Poker.* New York: Funk & Wagnalls, 1968.

20. Goren, C.H. *Goren's Bridge Complete.* Garden City, N.Y.: Doubleday, 1971.

Index

Aces
  optional value of, 4, 7–8
  separate count of, 113–119
  special rule for splitting, 9
"Action," defined, x
Amenities, 122, 154–155
Anchor man, 145
Any negative point count. *See*
  Minus-1 strategy
Archer point-count method, 37–
  44
  advantages of, xxi–xxii, 37, 50
  invention of, xxi–xxii, 34, 37
  refinements of counting, 47–
    49, 56–69
  summarized, 43–44
  See also Varying significance
    of point count

Baccarat, viii, 121, 135
Bad deck. *See* Minus-8 strategy

Baldwin group, xiii–xiv, 14, 170,
  180–181
  members, xiii
Baldwin, Roger, xiii. *See also* Baldwin group
Balinese Room, xix
Barring, 141, 148, 155
"Bases," defined, 3 (fig. 1), 68
Basic strategy, 14–33
  for doubling down, hard hands,
    21–24
  for doubling down, soft hands,
    24–27
  for splitting pairs, 27–30
  for standing or drawing, hard
    hands, 17–19
  for standing or drawing, soft
    hands, 19–21
  for surrender, 30–31
  summarized, 23 fig. 2, 32–33,
    103 table 1

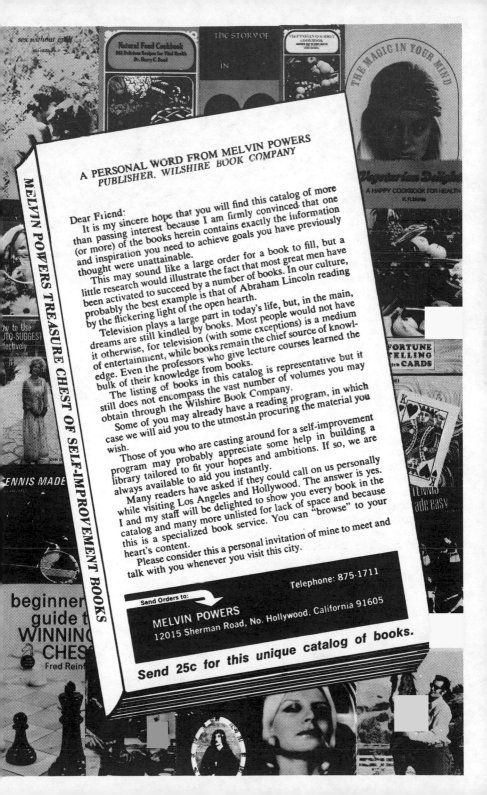

A PERSONAL WORD FROM MELVIN POWERS
PUBLISHER, WILSHIRE BOOK COMPANY

Dear Friend:

It is my sincere hope that you will find this catalog of more than passing interest because I am firmly convinced that one (or more) of the books herein contains exactly the information and inspiration you need to achieve goals you have previously thought were unattainable.

This may sound like a large order for a book to fill, but a little research would illustrate the fact that most great men have been activated to succeed by a number of books. In our culture, probably the best example is that of Abraham Lincoln reading by the flickering light of the open hearth.

Television plays a large part in today's life, but, in the main, dreams are still kindled by books. Most people would not have it otherwise, for television (with some exceptions) is a medium of entertainment, while books remain the chief source of knowledge. Even the professors who give lecture courses learned the bulk of their knowledge from books.

The listing of books in this catalog is representative but it still does not encompass the vast number of volumes you may obtain through the Wilshire Book Company.

Some of you may already have a reading program, in which case we will aid you to the utmost in procuring the material you wish.

Those of you who are casting around for a self-improvement program may probably appreciate some help in building a library tailored to fit your hopes and ambitions. If so, we are always available to aid you instantly.

Many readers have asked if they could call on us personally while visiting Los Angeles and Hollywood. The answer is yes. I and my staff will be delighted to show you every book in the catalog and many more unlisted for lack of space and because this is a specialized book service. You can "browse" to your heart's content.

Please consider this a personal invitation of mine to meet and talk with you whenever you visit this city.

Telephone: 875-1711

Send Orders to:

MELVIN POWERS
12015 Sherman Road, No. Hollywood, California 91605

Send 25c for this unique catalog of books.

Melvin Powers
SELF-IMPROVEMENT
LIBRARY

ASTROLOGY

_____ASTROLOGY: A FASCINATING HISTORY P. Naylor	2.00
_____ASTROLOGY: HOW TO CHART YOUR HOROSCOPE Max Heindel	2.00
_____ASTROLOGY: YOUR PERSONAL SUN-SIGN GUIDE Beatrice Ryder	3.00
_____ASTROLOGY FOR EVERYDAY LIVING Janet Harris	2.00
_____ASTROLOGY MADE EASY Astarte	2.00
_____ASTROLOGY MADE PRACTICAL Alexandra Kayhle	2.00
_____ASTROLOGY, ROMANCE, YOU AND THE STARS Anthony Norvell	3.00
_____MY WORLD OF ASTROLOGY Sydney Omarr	3.00
_____THOUGHT DIAL Sydney Omarr	2.00
_____ZODIAC REVEALED Rupert Gleadow	2.00

BRIDGE, POKER & GAMBLING

_____ADVANCED POKER STRATEGY & WINNING PLAY A. D. Livingston	2.00
_____BRIDGE BIDDING MADE EASY Edwin Kantar	5.00
_____BRIDGE CONVENTIONS Edwin Kantar	4.00
_____COMPLETE DEFENSIVE BRIDGE PLAY Edwin B. Kantar	10.00
_____HOW TO IMPROVE YOUR BRIDGE Alfred Sheinwold	2.00
_____HOW TO WIN AT DICE GAMES Skip Frey	2.00
_____HOW TO WIN AT POKER Terence Reese & Anthony T. Watkins	2.00
_____INTRODUCTION TO DEFENDER'S PLAY Edwin B. Kantar	3.00
_____SECRETS OF WINNING POKER George S. Coffin	3.00
_____TEST YOUR BRIDGE PLAY Edwin B. Kantar	3.00
_____WINNING AT 21 — An Expert's Guide John Archer	3.00

BUSINESS STUDY & REFERENCE

_____CONVERSATION MADE EASY Elliot Russell	2.00
_____EXAM SECRET Dennis B. Jackson	2.00
_____FIX-IT BOOK Arthur Symons	2.00
_____HOW TO DEVELOP A BETTER SPEAKING VOICE M. Hellier	2.00
_____HOW TO MAKE A FORTUNE IN REAL ESTATE Albert Winnikoff	3.00
_____HOW TO MAKE MONEY IN REAL ESTATE Stanley L. McMichael	2.00
_____INCREASE YOUR LEARNING POWER Geoffrey A. Dudley	2.00
_____MAGIC OF NUMBERS Robert Tocquet	2.00
_____PRACTICAL GUIDE TO BETTER CONCENTRATION Melvin Powers	2.00
_____PRACTICAL GUIDE TO PUBLIC SPEAKING Maurice Forley	2.00
_____7 DAYS TO FASTER READING William S. Schaill	2.00
_____SONGWRITERS' RHYMING DICTIONARY Jane Shaw Whitfield	3.00
_____SPELLING MADE EASY Lester D. Basch & Dr. Milton Finkelstein	2.00
_____STUDENT'S GUIDE TO BETTER GRADES J. A. Rickard	2.00
_____TEST YOURSELF — Find Your Hidden Talent Jack Shafer	2.00
_____YOUR WILL & WHAT TO DO ABOUT IT Attorney Samuel G. Kling	2.00

CHESS & CHECKERS

_____BEGINNER'S GUIDE TO WINNING CHESS Fred Reinfeld	2.00
_____BETTER CHESS — How to Play Fred Reinfeld	2.00
_____CHECKERS MADE EASY Tom Wiswell	2.00
_____CHESS IN TEN EASY LESSONS Larry Evans	2.00
_____CHESS MADE EASY Milton L. Hanauer	2.00

_____CHESS MASTERY — A New Approach *Fred Reinfeld* 2.00
_____CHESS PROBLEMS FOR BEGINNERS *edited by Fred Reinfeld* 2.00
_____CHESS SECRETS REVEALED *Fred Reinfeld* 2.00
_____CHESS STRATEGY — An Expert's Guide *Fred Reinfeld* 2.00
_____CHESS TACTICS FOR BEGINNERS *edited by Fred Reinfeld* 2.00
_____CHESS THEORY & PRACTICE *Morry & Mitchell* 2.00
_____HOW TO WIN AT CHECKERS *Fred Reinfeld* 2.00
_____1001 BRILLIANT WAYS TO CHECKMATE *Fred Reinfeld* 3.00
_____1001 WINNING CHESS SACRIFICES & COMBINATIONS *Fred Reinfeld* 3.00
_____SOVIET CHESS *Edited by R. G. Wade* 3.00

COOKERY & HERBS

_____CULPEPER'S HERBAL REMEDIES *Dr. Nicholas Culpeper* 2.00
_____FAST GOURMET COOKBOOK *Poppy Cannon* 2.50
_____HEALING POWER OF HERBS *May Bethel* 2.00
_____HERB HANDBOOK *Dawn MacLeod* 2.00
_____HERBS FOR COOKING AND HEALING *Dr. Donald Law* 2.00
_____HERBS FOR HEALTH How to Grow & Use Them *Louise Evans Doole* 2.00
_____HOME GARDEN COOKBOOK Delicious Natural Food Recipes *Ken Kraft* 3.00
_____MEDICAL HERBALIST *edited by Dr. J. R. Yemm* 3.00
_____NATURAL FOOD COOKBOOK *Dr. Harry C. Bond* 3.00
_____NATURE'S MEDICINES *Richard Lucas* 2.00
_____VEGETABLE GARDENING FOR BEGINNERS *Hugh Wiberg* 2.00
_____VEGETABLES FOR TODAY'S GARDENS *R. Milton Carleton* 2.00
_____VEGETARIAN COOKERY *Janet Walker* 3.00
_____VEGETARIAN COOKING MADE EASY & DELECTABLE *Veronica Vezza* 2.00
_____VEGETARIAN DELIGHTS — A Happy Cookbook for Health *K. R. Mehta* 2.00
_____VEGETARIAN GOURMET COOKBOOK *Joyce McKinnel* 2.00

HEALTH

_____DR. LINDNER'S SPECIAL WEIGHT CONTROL METHOD 1.00
_____HELP YOURSELF TO BETTER SIGHT *Margaret Darst Corbett* 3.00
_____HOW TO IMPROVE YOUR VISION *Dr. Robert A. Kraskin* 2.00
_____HOW YOU CAN STOP SMOKING PERMANENTLY *Ernest Caldwell* 2.00
_____LSD — THE AGE OF MIND *Bernard Roseman* 2.00
_____MIND OVER PLATTER *Peter G. Lindner, M.D.* 2.00
_____NEW CARBOHYDRATE DIET COUNTER *Patti Lopez-Pereira* 1.00
_____PSYCHEDELIC ECSTASY *William Marshall & Gilbert W. Taylor* 2.00
_____YOU CAN LEARN TO RELAX *Dr. Samuel Gutwirth* 2.00
_____YOUR ALLERGY—What To Do About It *Allan Knight, M.D.* 2.00

HOBBIES

_____BATON TWIRLING — A Complete Illustrated Guide *Doris Wheelus* 4.00
_____BEACHCOMBING FOR BEGINNERS *Norman Hickin* 2.00
_____BLACKSTONE'S MODERN CARD TRICKS *Harry Blackstone* 2.00
_____BLACKSTONE'S SECRETS OF MAGIC *Harry Blackstone* 2.00
_____COIN COLLECTING FOR BEGINNERS *Burton Hobson & Fred Reinfeld* 2.00
_____ENTERTAINING WITH ESP *Tony 'Doc' Shiels* 2.00
_____400 FASCINATING MAGIC TRICKS YOU CAN DO *Howard Thurston* 3.00
_____GOULD'S GOLD & SILVER GUIDE TO COINS *Maurice Gould* 2.00
_____HOW I TURN JUNK INTO FUN AND PROFIT *Sari* 3.00
_____HOW TO WRITE A HIT SONG & SELL IT *Tommy Boyce* 7.00
_____JUGGLING MADE EASY *Rudolf Dittrich* 2.00
_____MAGIC MADE EASY *Byron Wels* 2.00
_____SEW SIMPLY, SEW RIGHT *Mini Rhea & F. Leighton* 2.00
_____STAMP COLLECTING FOR BEGINNERS *Burton Hobson* 2.00
_____STAMP COLLECTING FOR FUN & PROFIT *Frank Cetin* 2.00

HORSE PLAYERS' WINNING GUIDES

_____BETTING HORSES TO WIN *Les Conklin* 2.00
_____ELIMINATE THE LOSERS *Bob McKnight* 2.00
_____HOW TO PICK WINNING HORSES *Bob McKnight* 2.00
_____HOW TO WIN AT THE RACES *Sam (The Genius) Lewin* 2.00

_____HOW YOU CAN BEAT THE RACES *Jack Kavanagh*   2.00
_____MAKING MONEY AT THE RACES *David Barr*   2.00
_____PAYDAY AT THE RACES *Les Conklin*   2.00
_____SMART HANDICAPPING MADE EASY *William Bauman*   2.00
_____SUCCESS AT THE HARNESS RACES *Barry Meadow*   2.50
_____WINNING AT THE HARNESS RACES—An Expert's Guide *Nick Cammarano* 2.50

HUMOR
_____BILL BALLANCE HANDBOOK OF NIFTY MOVES *Bill Ballance*   3.00
_____HOW TO BE A COMEDIAN FOR FUN & PROFIT *King & Laufer* 2.00
_____JOKE TELLER'S HANDBOOK *Bob Orben*   2.00

HYPNOTISM
_____ADVANCED TECHNIQUES OF HYPNOSIS *Melvin Powers*   2.00
_____CHILDBIRTH WITH HYPNOSIS *William S. Kroger, M.D.*   2.00
_____HOW TO SOLVE YOUR SEX PROBLEMS
    WITH SELF-HYPNOSIS *Frank S. Caprio, M.D.*   2.00
_____HOW TO STOP SMOKING THRU SELF-HYPNOSIS *Leslie M. LeCron* 2.00
_____HOW TO USE AUTO-SUGGESTION EFFECTIVELY *John Duckworth* 2.00
_____HOW YOU CAN BOWL BETTER USING SELF-HYPNOSIS *Jack Heise* 2.00
_____HOW YOU CAN PLAY BETTER GOLF USING SELF-HYPNOSIS *Heise* 2.00
_____HYPNOSIS AND SELF-HYPNOSIS *Bernard Hollander, M.D.* 2.00
_____HYPNOTISM (*Originally published in 1893*) *Carl Sextus* 3.00
_____HYPNOTISM & PSYCHIC PHENOMENA *Simeon Edwards*   3.00
_____HYPNOTISM MADE EASY *Dr. Ralph Winn*   2.00
_____HYPNOTISM MADE PRACTICAL *Louis Orton*   2.00
_____HYPNOTISM REVEALED *Melvin Powers*   1.00
_____HYPNOTISM TODAY *Leslie LeCron & Jean Bordeaux, Ph.D.* 2.00
_____MODERN HYPNOSIS *Lesley Kuhn & Salvatore Russo, Ph.D.* 3.00
_____NEW CONCEPTS OF HYPNOSIS *Bernard C. Gindes, M.D.*   3.00
_____POST-HYPNOTIC INSTRUCTIONS *Arnold Furst*   3.00
    How to give post-hypnotic suggestions for therapeutic purposes.
_____PRACTICAL GUIDE TO SELF-HYPNOSIS *Melvin Powers*   2.00
_____PRACTICAL HYPNOTISM *Philip Magonet, M.D.*   2.00
_____SECRETS OF HYPNOTISM *S. J. Van Pelt, M.D.*   3.00
_____SELF-HYPNOSIS *Paul Adams*   3.00
_____SELF-HYPNOSIS Its Theory, Technique & Application *Melvin Powers* 2.00
_____SELF-HYPNOSIS A Conditioned-Response Technique *Laurance Sparks* 3.00
_____THERAPY THROUGH HYPNOSIS *edited by Raphael H. Rhodes* 3.00

JUDAICA
_____HOW TO LIVE A RICHER & FULLER LIFE *Rabbi Edgar F. Magnin* 2.00
_____MODERN ISRAEL *Lily Edelman*   2.00
_____OUR JEWISH HERITAGE *Rabbi Alfred Wolf & Joseph Gaer* 2.00
_____ROMANCE OF HASSIDISM *Jacob S. Minkin*   2.50
_____SERVICE OF THE HEART *Evelyn Garfield, Ph.D.*   3.00
_____STORY OF ISRAEL IN COINS *Jean & Maurice Gould*   2.00
_____STORY OF ISRAEL IN STAMPS *Maxim & Gabriel Shamir*   1.00
_____TONGUE OF THE PROPHETS *Robert St. John*   3.00
_____TREASURY OF COMFORT *edited by Rabbi Sidney Greenberg* 3.00

MARRIAGE, SEX & PARENTHOOD
_____ABILITY TO LOVE *Dr. Allan Fromme*   3.00
_____ENCYCLOPEDIA OF MODERN SEX & LOVE TECHNIQUES *Macandrew* 3.00
_____GUIDE TO SUCCESSFUL MARRIAGE *Drs. Albert Ellis & Robert Harper* 3.00
_____HOW TO RAISE AN EMOTIONALLY HEALTHY, HAPPY CHILD, *A. Ellis* 2.00
_____IMPOTENCE & FRIGIDITY *Edwin W. Hirsch, M.D.*   3.00
_____JUST FOR WOMEN — A Guide to the Female Body *Richard E. Sand, M.D.* 3.00
_____NEW APPROACHES TO SEX IN MARRIAGE *John E. Eichenlaub, M.D.* 3.00
_____SEX WITHOUT GUILT *Albert Ellis, Ph.D.*   2.00
_____SEXUALLY ADEQUATE FEMALE *Frank S. Caprio, M.D.*   2.00
_____SEXUALLY ADEQUATE MALE *Frank S. Caprio, M.D.*   2.00
_____YOUR FIRST YEAR OF MARRIAGE *Dr. Tom McGinnis*   2.00

METAPHYSICS & OCCULT

_____BOOK OF TALISMANS, AMULETS & ZODIACAL GEMS William Pavitt	3.00
_____CONCENTRATION—A Guide to Mental Mastery Mouni Sadhu	3.00
_____DREAMS & OMENS REVEALED Fred Gettings	2.00
_____EXTRASENSORY PERCEPTION Simeon Edmunds	2.00
_____EXTRA-TERRESTRIAL INTELLIGENCE—The First Encounter	6.00
_____FORTUNE TELLING WITH CARDS P. Foli	2.00
_____HANDWRITING ANALYSIS MADE EASY John Marley	2.00
_____HANDWRITING TELLS Nadya Olyanova	3.00
_____HOW TO UNDERSTAND YOUR DREAMS Geoffrey A. Dudley	2.00
_____ILLUSTRATED YOGA William Zorn	2.00
_____IN DAYS OF GREAT PEACE Mouni Sadhu	3.00
_____KING SOLOMON'S TEMPLE IN THE MASONIC TRADITION Alex Horne	5.00
_____MAGICIAN — His training and work W. E. Butler	2.00
_____MEDITATION Mouni Sadhu	3.00
_____MODERN NUMEROLOGY Morris C. Goodman	2.00
_____NUMEROLOGY—ITS FACTS AND SECRETS Ariel Yvon Taylor	2.00
_____PALMISTRY MADE EASY Fred Gettings	2.00
_____PALMISTRY MADE PRACTICAL Elizabeth Daniels Squire	3.00
_____PALMISTRY SECRETS REVEALED Henry Frith	2.00
_____PRACTICAL YOGA Ernest Wood	3.00
_____PROPHECY IN OUR TIME Martin Ebon	2.50
_____PSYCHOLOGY OF HANDWRITING Nadya Olyanova	3.00
_____SEEING INTO THE FUTURE Harvey Day	2.00
_____SUPERSTITION — Are you superstitious? Eric Maple	2.00
_____TAROT Mouni Sadhu	4.00
_____TAROT OF THE BOHEMIANS Papus	3.00
_____TEST YOUR ESP Martin Ebon	2.00
_____WAYS TO SELF-REALIZATION Mouni Sadhu	2.00
_____WITCHCRAFT, MAGIC & OCCULTISM—A Fascinating History W. B. Crow	3.00
_____WITCHCRAFT — THE SIXTH SENSE Justine Glass	2.00
_____WORLD OF PSYCHIC RESEARCH Hereward Carrington	2.00
_____YOU CAN ANALYZE HANDWRITING Robert Holder	2.00

SELF-HELP & INSPIRATIONAL

_____CYBERNETICS WITHIN US Y. Saparina	3.00
_____DAILY POWER FOR JOYFUL LIVING Dr. Donald Curtis	2.00
_____DOCTOR PSYCHO-CYBERNETICS Maxwell Maltz, M.D.	3.00
_____DYNAMIC THINKING Melvin Powers	1.00
_____GREATEST POWER IN THE UNIVERSE U. S. Andersen	4.00
_____GROW RICH WHILE YOU SLEEP Ben Sweetland	2.00
_____GROWTH THROUGH REASON Albert Ellis, Ph.D.	3.00
_____GUIDE TO DEVELOPING YOUR POTENTIAL Herbert A. Otto, Ph.D.	3.00
_____GUIDE TO LIVING IN BALANCE Frank S. Caprio, M.D.	2.00
_____HELPING YOURSELF WITH APPLIED PSYCHOLOGY R. Henderson	2.00
_____HELPING YOURSELF WITH PSYCHIATRY Frank S. Caprio, M.D.	2.00
_____HOW TO ATTRACT GOOD LUCK A. H. Z. Carr	2.00
_____HOW TO CONTROL YOUR DESTINY Norvell	2.00
_____HOW TO DEVELOP A WINNING PERSONALITY Martin Panzer	3.00
_____HOW TO DEVELOP AN EXCEPTIONAL MEMORY Young & Gibson	3.00
_____HOW TO OVERCOME YOUR FEARS M. P. Leahy, M.D.	2.00
_____HOW YOU CAN HAVE CONFIDENCE AND POWER Les Giblin	2.00
_____HUMAN PROBLEMS & HOW TO SOLVE THEM Dr. Donald Curtis	2.00
_____I CAN Ben Sweetland	3.00
_____I WILL Ben Sweetland	2.00
_____LEFT-HANDED PEOPLE Michael Barsley	3.00
_____MAGIC IN YOUR MIND U. S. Andersen	3.00
_____MAGIC OF THINKING BIG Dr. David J. Schwartz	2.00
_____MAGIC POWER OF YOUR MIND Walter M. Germain	3.00
_____MENTAL POWER THRU SLEEP SUGGESTION Melvin Powers	1.00
_____NEW GUIDE TO RATIONAL LIVING Albert Ellis, Ph.D. - R. Harper, Ph.D.	3.00
_____OUR TROUBLED SELVES Dr. Allan Fromme	3.00
_____PRACTICAL GUIDE TO SUCCESS & POPULARITY C. W. Bailey	

_____PSYCHO-CYBERNETICS *Maxwell Maltz, M.D.*   2.00
_____SCIENCE OF MIND IN DAILY LIVING *Dr. Donald Curtis*   2.00
_____SECRET OF SECRETS *U. S. Andersen*   3.00
_____STUTTERING AND WHAT YOU CAN DO ABOUT IT *W. Johnson, Ph.D.*   2.00
_____SUCCESS-CYBERNETICS *U. S. Andersen*   3.00
_____10 DAYS TO A GREAT NEW LIFE *William E. Edwards*   2.00
_____THINK AND GROW RICH *Napoleon Hill*   3.00
_____THREE MAGIC WORDS *U. S. Andersen*   3.00
_____TREASURY OF THE ART OF LIVING *Sidney S. Greenberg*   3.00
_____YOU ARE NOT THE TARGET *Laura Huxley*   3.00
_____YOUR SUBCONSCIOUS POWER *Charles M. Simmons*   3.00
_____YOUR THOUGHTS CAN CHANGE YOUR LIFE *Dr. Donald Curtis*   2.00

SPORTS

_____ARCHERY — An Expert's Guide *Don Stamp*   2.00
_____BICYCLING FOR FUN AND GOOD HEALTH *Kenneth E. Luther*   2.00
_____BILLIARDS—Pocket • Carom • Three Cushion *Clive Cottingham, Jr.*   2.00
_____CAMPING-OUT 101 Ideas & Activities *Bruno Knobel*   2.00
_____COMPLETE GUIDE TO FISHING *Vlad Evanoff*   2.00
_____HOW TO WIN AT POCKET BILLIARDS *Edward D. Knuchell*   3.00
_____MOTORCYCLING FOR BEGINNERS *I. G. Edmonds*   2.00
_____PRACTICAL BOATING *W. S. Kals*   3.00
_____SECRET OF BOWLING STRIKES *Dawson Taylor*   2.00
_____SECRET OF PERFECT PUTTING *Horton Smith & Dawson Taylor*   2.00
_____SECRET WHY FISH BITE *James Westman*   2.00
_____SKIER'S POCKET BOOK *Otti Wiedman* (4¼" x 6")   2.50
_____SOCCER—The game & how to play it *Gary Rosenthal*   2.00
_____TABLE TENNIS MADE EASY *Johnny Leach*   2.00

TENNIS LOVERS' LIBRARY

_____BEGINNER'S GUIDE TO WINNING TENNIS *Helen Hull Jacobs*   2.00
_____HOW TO BEAT BETTER TENNIS PLAYERS *Loring Fiske*   3.00
_____HOW TO IMPROVE YOUR TENNIS—Style, Strategy & Analysis *C. Wilson*   2.00
_____PLAY TENNIS WITH ROSEWALL *Ken Rosewall*   2.00
_____PSYCH YOURSELF TO BETTER TENNIS *Dr. Walter A. Luszki*   2.00
_____SUCCESSFUL TENNIS *Neale Fraser*   2.00
_____TENNIS FOR BEGINNERS *Dr. H. A. Murray*   2.00
_____TENNIS MADE EASY *Joel Brecheen*   2.00
_____WEEKEND TENNIS—How to have fun & win at the same time *Bill Talbert*   2.00
_____WINNING WITH PERCENTAGE TENNIS *Jack Lowe*   2.00
    An Expert's Guide to Smart Court Strategy & Technique

WILSHIRE MINIATURE LIBRARY (4¼" x 6" in full color)

_____BUTTERFLIES   2.50
_____LIPIZZANERS & THE SPANISH RIDING SCHOOL   2.50
_____SKIER'S POCKET BOOK   2.50

WILSHIRE PET LIBRARY

_____DOG OBEDIENCE TRAINING *Gust Kessopulos*   2.00
_____DOG TRAINING MADE EASY & FUN *John W. Kellogg*   2.00
_____HOW TO BRING UP YOUR PET DOG *Kurt Unkelbach*   2.00
_____HOW TO RAISE & TRAIN YOUR PUPPY *Jeff Griffen*   2.00
_____PIGEONS: HOW TO RAISE & TRAIN THEM *William H. Allen, Jr.*   2.00

The books listed above can be obtained from your book dealer or directly from Melvin Powers. When ordering, please remit 25c per book postage & handling. Send 25c for our illustrated catalog of self-improvement books.

Melvin Powers

12015 Sherman Road, No. Hollywood, California 91605

Notes

Notes